MW00334937

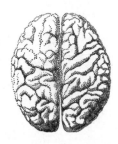

PRAISE FOR *THRIVE BY DESIGN*

"Get *Thrive By Design*, a graduate course in employee engagement in a compelling, well-crafted read chock-full of immediately actionable content. The micro-learning video courses we have created based on Don's work tops our ratings. Incredible insight and a completely fresh take on leadership—an essential read for any leader or manager serious about their craft."

—**Steve Meyer**, CEO, Rapid Learning Institute

"Construction is a tough business, and nothing is more challenging than creating the right work environment where great people come together and perform at their best. We are constructing a culture that has allowed us to flourish even on the most demanding projects. Culture is king in our mind, and the insights in *Thrive By Design* have captured the hearts and minds of our top leaders."

—**Craig Weems**, COO, Sunland Asphalt

"When I experienced firsthand the impact of a science-based approach to creating a workplace where employees look forward to coming to work, I was all in. The depth of understanding on what drives the daily performance of our employees has been revelatory. The hands-on insights in *Thrive by Design* are a breath of fresh air in the otherwise stale atmosphere of leadership advice."

—**Els Thurmote**, CEO, TVH Americas

"Most of us at SEH are engineers, architects, scientists, and planners, and we knew we needed more than Gantt charts and flow diagrams to move our culture to a new level. The practical advice laid out in *Thrive by Design* as implemented by Don and his team has moved our culture to a demonstrably better place. Turnover is down and performance is up. We are much better positioned for attracting and retaining the best talent and solving client challenges."

—**Sam Claassen**, CEO, Short Elliott Hendrickson Inc. (SEH)

THRIVE
BY DESIGN

THRIVE

BY DESIGN

THE NEUROSCIENCE THAT DRIVES
HIGH-PERFORMANCE CULTURES

DON RHEEM

ForbesBooks

Published by ForbesBooks, Charleston, South Carolina.
Member of Advantage Media Group.

ForbesBooks is a registered trademark, and the ForbesBooks colophon is a trademark of Forbes Media, LLC.

Printed in the United States of America.

10 9 8 7 6 5 4 3 2

ISBN: 978-1-946633-06-4
LCCN: 2017942458

Cover design by Katie Biondo.
Layout design by Megan Elger.

This publication is designed to provide accurate and authoritative information in regard to the subject matter covered. It is sold with the understanding that the publisher is not engaged in rendering legal, accounting, or other professional services. If legal advice or other expert assistance is required, the services of a competent professional person should be sought.

Advantage Media Group is proud to be a part of the Tree Neutral® program. Tree Neutral offsets the number of trees consumed in the production and printing of this book by taking proactive steps such as planting trees in direct proportion to the number of trees used to print books. To learn more about Tree Neutral, please visit **www.treeneutral.com.**

Since 1917, the Forbes mission has remained constant. Global Champions of Entrepreneurial Capitalism. ForbesBooks exists to further that aim by bringing the Stories, Passion, and Knowledge of top thought leaders to the forefront. ForbesBooks brings you The Best in Business. To be considered for publication, please visit **www.forbesbooks.com.**

In dedication to my remarkable wife, Kathryn, and equally remarkable daughters, Jocelyn and Marisa, for helping me understand what true relational leadership should be. And to my parents, Patricia and Bill, who led the way for personal discovery.

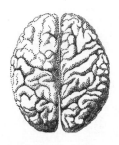

TABLE OF CONTENTS

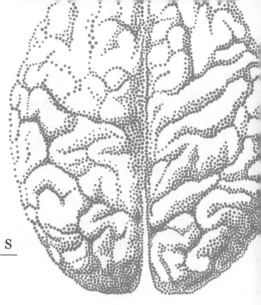

ACKNOWLEDGMENTS

As every author knows, books don't just appear. The idea might, but the words that hit the page come from countless experiences, assists, mentors, close colleagues, and friends. I am blessed with an abundance of these experiential and relational assets, and this is a unique opportunity to both reflect and express some gratitude to the intellectual and emotional underpinnings of this book.

As you will read in these pages, having safe and secure connections with others is perhaps the most life-sustaining nutrient for our species. Without the early friendships with key individuals who demonstrated outstanding character, I don't think the path I took to this book would have existed. So let me thank Ed Rempalski, Jacki Stewart Felvy, Jim Stark, Russ Miller, and John Mitchell.

Mentors are another critical source of knowledge, course correction, and flat-out admiration. My life was significantly influenced by personal guidance from Ken Bechtel, Dr. John F. Wanamaker, Dr. Jerry Collester, and E. Bruce Harrison. My grandfather, Richard S. Rheem, founder of Rheem Manufacturing, turned a barrel factory into an international brand known for excellence and innovation in heating and air conditioning equipment. He and my father, William

S. Rheem, taught me early lessons on business growth and the importance of high-character leadership.

Early professional experiences were also formative for this book. As a technical consultant to the Science, Technology, and Space Committee in the US House of Representatives and subsequently as a science advisor to the Secretary of the Department of Health and Human Services, I quickly learned about the politics of science and how vital the application of solid science can be on social policy and human well-being.

My brilliant wife, Dr. Kathryn Rheem, a marriage and family therapist and director of the Washington Baltimore Center for Emotionally Focused Therapy, has not only introduced me to the science of adult attachment but also to some of the remarkable leaders in the field. Her introductions to luminaries like Dr. Susan Johnson (director of the International Centre for Excellence in Emotionally Focused Therapy) and Dr. James Coan (associate professor of clinical psychology and director of the Virginia Affective Neuroscience Laboratory at the University of Virginia) and the hours I have spent with each of them inspired both this book and the creation of my company, E3 Solutions.

If I have any writing skills, I owe a debt of gratitude to the Christian Science Monitor, one of the world's truly great journalistic institutions that allowed me to cover beats in science, technology, politics, and ultimately the White House. The text that follows has been resurrected from my pedestrian prose to something readable by the extraordinary editorial skills of Kelly Sargent Burns, who has patiently and laboriously reviewed every word. Laurie Nappi and Rebecca Hantman on my E3 team also reviewed key parts of the text. Christina White and Dan Pettine provided research assistance. Corie Luzon, Scott Neville, and Keith Kopcsak at ForbesBooks both inspired and cajoled the writing process for which I am very appreciative.

And finally, I must acknowledge the critical lessons and insights I have learned from the hundreds of CEOs in the US, Canada, and Great Britain that I have worked and met with over the last decade in my role as consultant and advisor. It was the constant question, "Do you have this written down in a book?" that led me to do just that. It seemed like such a simple idea . . .

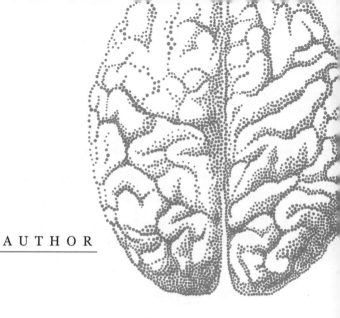

Don Rheem is CEO of E3 Solutions, a provider of employee workplace metrics that allow organizations to build engaged, high-performance cultures. Rheem focuses on using science-backed research in consulting with leaders at all levels within an organization.

Rheem and his team show business leaders how to create the workplace conditions that trigger hardwired motivators that improve employee performance. These intrinsic drivers of human behavior increase employee engagement in ways that improve productivity, positivity, team alignment, morale, and retention.

A former science advisor to both the US Congress and the secretary of the Department of Health and Human Services, Rheem shares with clients a grounded and empirically validated methodology to get employees more engaged and better positioned for bottom-line success.

Rheem has more than thirty years of experience helping organizations derive more value and impact from everyday business functions. His clients include Honeywell, Bank of America, Corporation for Public Broadcasting, National Institutes of Health (NIH), Smithfield Foods, Major League Baseball, Discovery Channel, LexisNexis, Green Mountain Coffee, and many other national brands and nonprofits.

He has coached US senators, royalty, and thousands of CEOs and senior executives in the private and nonprofit sectors.

A former White House correspondent for the Christian Science Monitor with a background in science, technology, and politics, Rheem is also an award-winning public affairs executive. He served as a technical consultant to the Committee on Science, Space, and Technology in the US House of Representatives, advising members on public policy issues, including basic scientific research. Rheem comes from a long line of entrepreneurs; his great-grandfather built the first oil refinery on the west coast before becoming president of Standard Oil and his grandfather was the founder of Rheem manufacturing, once a Fortune 200 company and still one of the largest suppliers of water heaters and air conditioning equipment in the world.

A popular speaker and thought leader, Rheem lectures throughout North America and Europe on increasing employee engagement, helping thousands of CEOs understand the primary drivers of exceptional workplace behavior. Rheem lives just outside of Washington, DC, with his wife, Dr. Kathryn Rheem, and in his free time he enjoys writing and spending time with his family.

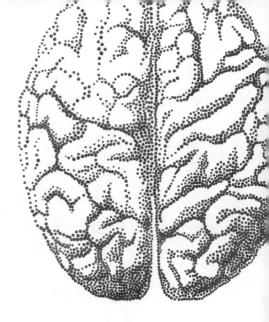

Executives and managers are under unprecedented pressure to produce improved results in what have become the most fast-paced, complex workplace conditions in history. This complexity stems from a myriad of factors, such as a growing reliance on data collection and analysis, evaporating administrative support, and disruptive change in areas across the board, including in materials, design, and manufacture. At the same time, leaders at all levels are witnessing a steady decline in talent (employees with the competency to do the work well), a millennial generation (now the largest segment of the US labor pool) that expects more from employers than just a paycheck, grueling global competition, increasing government oversight and regulation, and the list goes on. Never has the recipe for organizational success been more complicated, and no ingredient is more critical to that success than the people who go to work every day. How employees show up—either engaged and volunteering their discretionary effort or simply doing the minimum—will determine the truly great companies going forward.

As human beings, our most compelling need is for connection. Clinical evidence and research in neuroscience and social science reveals the unambiguous benefits of working in groups and having safe and secure connections with others. Through this research, the clear picture that emerges is of a species biologically driven to work together and share the load, leveraging strong relationships for mutual benefit.[1]

There is overwhelming evidence that we are hardwired to perform at our best in a group—what historically was a clan or a tribe. Today, the workplace fulfills that neural hunger. Work is where adults in the Western world spend most of their time (while awake) with other adults.

In my organization, we operate on the understanding that because humans are herd animals, we are hardwired from birth to connect with others—and for most of us that is a key driver and benefit of going to work. As savvy leaders will come to understand in the coming decades, landing a *great job* will be defined more by how it feels than by how it pays.

AS SAVVY LEADERS WILL COME TO UNDERSTAND IN THE COMING DECADES, LANDING A GREAT JOB WILL BE DEFINED MORE BY HOW IT FEELS THAN BY HOW IT PAYS.

At E3 Solutions, where I serve as founder and CEO, our approach to creating high-performance workplace cultures is unique. We use empirically validated science to construct a methodology that consistently and predictably improves the quality and the expression of employee behavior. Not only can we prove that our approach works, I explain why employees are more engaged (productive, focused, fulfilled) as a result. The benefits radiate beyond the individual to the

---

1   Specifically referring to Dr. John Bowlby's attachment theory, Dr. Susan Johnson's work in emotionally focused couple therapy, neuroscientist/clinical psychologist Dr. James Coan's social baseline theory, and the prosocial research aptly covered by Dr. Laura Padilla-Walker and Dr. Gustavo Carlo in their book *Prosocial Development*.

team, the department, and the organization. The key is in the biological hardwiring of humans—a neurological imperative that makes certain conditions universal drivers of high-level performance, now frequently referred to as employee engagement.

At E3 we focus on the systems, leadership skill sets, and environments that encourage engagement, based on new insights into what allows the brain to thrive. Unfortunately, the conditions that exist inside typical workplace cultures are rarely aligned with this understanding of what nurtures great performance. In this book, I want to help leaders at all levels in the organization understand the conditions in which the brain will "thrive by design." When these conditions are created in workplace cultures, whether by the CEO across the organization or by managers within their teams, employee engagement increases. This is not about motivational posters and free lunches. It's about organizations being more intentional with their cultures. It's about creating the conditions the brain has looked for every day since birth in order to have meaningful and trusted relationships.

When leaders move their culture in the direction we recommend, employees behave with higher levels of mental acuity, productivity, and fulfillment, among a host of other pro-engagement outcomes. We know, for example, that a better model for engaging employees is based on positive, constructive feedback and more frequent validation and recognition. While not the total story, shifting to a more positive mindset and a positive leadership model is just one approach where the research shows remarkable results.

It is also essential for business leaders to find better ways to connect and engage millennials and Gen Z employees, who tend to frame work in distinctly different ways than preceding generations. In chapter 1, we will explain why the old leadership style, typically hierarchical and punitive ("I may have to write you up . . ."), simply won't work like it used to. Members of the youngest (and largest) segment of the US workforce are demanding more from their leaders and the overall experience of work, and in the pages that follow you will discover an effective road map for how to interact more effectively in what I refer to as the *mindset economy*, where employees want to find meaning and purpose between, rather than within, the weekends.

I also talk about adult attachment theory, especially in chapter 2, "Relationship Science." Seven decades of research on adult attachment show that, as human beings, not only are we hardwired to be in a group but, more specifically, we also need to have safe and secure connections on a personal or intimate basis. The work of Dr. Susan Johnson, director of the International Centre for Excellence in Emotionally Focused Therapy, is nothing short of remarkable and is the foundation of this chapter.

What you will find in the pages that follow are some very practical approaches to outperforming your competition. As business leaders begin to realize that the nascent talent shortages so many companies are now facing are actually permanent—and will only get worse over time—everyone will be rushing to create compelling workplace cultures in order to attract and keep the best talent possible. But when everyone is doing the same thing at the same time (no matter how efficacious), your early adopter advantage is lost.

In this book, you will get suggested interventions on how to build better, healthier, and more engaged workplace cultures. You will also gain invaluable insights into *why* these interventions work. You've heard the saying "Give a man a fish and he eats for a day; teach him to fish and he eats for a lifetime." I want today's leaders to have a much better understanding of what people need in order to thrive. With that knowledge, you can create your own interventions!

I also share a hardwired relational narrative created by our species centuries ago whose importance we are only now beginning to understand. This narrative is the ultimate behavioral "big picture" because it reveals a context for just about everything we do behaviorally. By engaging your employees, you can increase productivity, share your passion, and help your organization thrive. Read on and you'll see that this new relational science will be the key distinguishing characteristic of tomorrow's model companies.

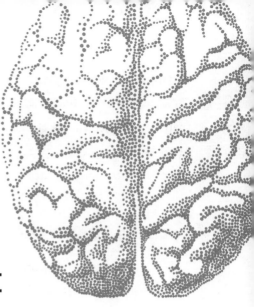

CHAPTER 1

THE WORKPLACE HAS EVOLVED

For most of human history, the only instrument needed to induce employees to complete their duties energetically and adroitly was the whip.[2]

—ALAIN DE BOTTON

There is no question that the demands on leaders have never been more sophisticated and complex than they are today. Whether it's managing the supply chain, using a new suite of workplace analytics, or dealing with automation, quality control, or employee performance, the span of talents needed to be a successful manager and leader is increasing. Management at all levels needs new and better skills to cope with these growing challenges.[3]

In the geography of today's workplace, tectonic shifts are in motion that will subduct many of the old ways of managing people beneath a healthier surface plate of workplace engagement. In this

---

2   Alain de Botton, *The Pleasures and Sorrows of Work* (New York: Vintage, 2010).

3   Marco Nink and Jennifer Robison, "Can Bad Managers Be Saved?" *Gallup Business Journal,* December 21, 2016.

chapter, we will look at two overarching trends that will shape the new workplace—first, a seismic shift in the availability of talent and labor, and second, an equally profound shift in the mindset of the new talent pool. We will also examine what the new needs will be for leaders who want to outperform the competition.

WORKPLACE 1.0–2.0

As a conceptual framework, let's break the postindustrial workplace into three general eras. **Workplace 1.0** took place roughly from 1815 to the late 1960s. A significant marker of this era was that there were always more people than jobs, so those who had work were motivated in large part by the fear of being fired. In this abundant labor market, there was very little attention paid to workers beyond their general job competence and productivity. For baby boomers, their parents, and grandparents, the predominant lens through which they saw work was the need to get a job and keep it. Indeed, economic survival in the twentieth century was primarily linked to having secure employment. In this kind of environment, it was far more important to have a job than it was to enjoy the work or to find meaning in it. As my grandfather, Richard S. Rheem, built Rheem manufacturing into one of the largest manufacturers of water heaters, heating, and air conditioning in the world, employees were in abundance, and very little time was spent on slackers. There was a regular line at the Rheem employment office on just about every job site. The employees that Rheem hired were grateful for the job and strove to keep it; employee family finances were razor thin—there was no margin for failure.

Workplace 2.0 followed and will likely continue for another decade or so, depending on labor availability and the economy. A combination of robust economic growth and a decline in available talent would shorten this transitional era, in which organizations are facing exponential shifts not only in markets and technology but also in how they lead, engage, and keep their workforce. Company values and culture are emerging as competitive differentiators for employees (and customers), especially in the technology and software fields related to smart devices, artificial intelligence, and robotics. We have also seen this play out with increasingly popular companies that have a strong social entrepreneurship focus, such as TOMS shoes, Warby Parker, and the like. Workplace 2.0 is where we start to see a bifurcation of struggling leaders and effective leaders. Struggling leaders look back fondly on the "good old days" of command-and-control management where employees came to work simply out of obligation. Effective leaders, however, welcome a new era where staff members look forward to coming to a workplace that is positive—where collaboration and a relational mindset are as important as accountability and performance metrics.

AGE OF COMPLIANCE

I think of the Workplace 1.0 era as the *Age of Compliance*—a time when employees needed to comply with whatever conditions were offered in order to keep their job. If an employee couldn't comply with the terms of the job, they would typically be fired and replaced with a willing-to-comply new employee just grateful to get a regular paycheck and a better chance at the American Dream.

The Age of Compliance was relatively easy on managers for this reason; people came to work because they had to—they had few, if any, choices. A manager's primary responsibility was making sure everyone showed up and delivered a decent day's work for a decent day's pay. Managers didn't have to have a particularly robust leadership skill set in order to do the job. If a seasoned employee worked hard and was fairly responsible, he or she could be promoted to a manager. Tenure, not skill set, was—and to a large extent still is—the primary reason employees are lifted into management. It didn't matter if employees didn't like their manager, because they really had no choice. They worked for the manager not because that person was a great leader but because he or she was the boss.

Let's contrast this Age of Compliance to where we are headed over the next ten to twenty years at the tail end of Workplace 2.0. Because of a declining rate of labor growth in combination with an increasing level of skill needed to perform well in a postindustrial economy, finding talent has become increasingly difficult. Not only will there be a declining rate of new job entrants, but the skill sets needed to accomplish the work will be harder to find. Our clients are already finding themselves in the enviable position of having growing markets but with a debilitating inability to fill positions needed to meet that growth.

Strategic affairs expert George Friedman reflects on this issue in his book *The Next 100 Years: A Forecast for the 21st Century*: "Quite simply, in the first half of the century, the population bust will create a major labor shortage in advanced industrial countries. Today, developed countries see the problem as keeping immigrants out. Later in the first half of the twenty-first century, the problem will be persuading them to come. Countries will go so far as to pay people to move there."[4]

Just as nations must adapt to new geopolitical realities, business must also adjust to pervasive changes in the labor landscape. The

---

4   George Friedman, *The Next 100 Years: A Forecast for the 21st Century* (New York: Doubleday, 2009), p. 9.

business press likes to talk of *disruptive* new technologies (smart-phones, Uber); in the future, the same word will be used by econo-mists and historians as they describe the massive shift in the way business treats employees over the coming decade. We have seen similar seismic shifts in the business world before. The advent of railroads changed the early American economy, just as the inter-state highway system created a modern transportation infrastructure that changed the way businesses could operate. The broad use of computers in business and at home is another obvious major shift in the nature and daily functioning of our economy.

The shift we now face is driven by the fact that we are approach-ing the cliff edge of the most severe labor shortage we have faced since World War II, only this one isn't short term. Headlines like *The Wall Street Journal*'s "America's Growing Labor Shortage"—in this case lamenting the looming worker shortage in the construction and agricultural sectors—will multiply.[5] The day after that headline appeared, *USA Today* led the business section with an article describ-ing a 1.4 million shortfall in software development employees by 2020.[6] Declining rates of labor growth across the industrialized world are not going to change, and the result will be a talent war as organi-zations compete to find employees with the appropriate skill sets to meet the demands of economic growth, prosperity, and the growing complexity of work. This isn't just a high-tech issue; the CEOs I work with complain of shortages across the board—machinists, welders, coders, social media specialists, and more.

Additionally, the population in the industrialized world is shrink-ing.[7] Economists explain that the primary reason for this reduction is

---

5 "America's Growing Labor Shortage," *The Wall Street Journal,* March 30, 2017.

6 "Plenty of Tech Jobs, But . . . Few Workers Who Have the Chops," *USA Today,* March 31, 2017.

7 "Population Decline and the Great Economic Reversal," Stratfor Enterprises, February 17, 2015, https://www.stratfor.com/weekly/population-decline-and-great-economic-reversal.

that children—once considered valuable economic assets at as young as six or seven in a preindustrial world—have now become economic liabilities in a postindustrial world. Instead of materially contributing at a young age, there is very little children can offer to offset their expenses. These costs are not trivial; recent government data put the average cost of raising a child (born in America in 2013) until age eighteen at $245,340. If you adjust for projected inflation, that number increases to $304,480.[8] And that is before adding in the cost of a college education. The point is, the more expensive children became, the less likely families were to want—or be able to afford—more of them.[9]

WORKPLACE 3.0: THE AGE OF CHOICE

The challenge is even more complex than simply labor scarcity. As baby boomers retire, the proportion of younger workers is rapidly expanding, and that creates its own tectonic shifts in the workforce. Millennials (adults aged twenty to thirty-five in 2017) now represent more than half of the American workforce, and that proportion will continue to grow over the next decade. In 2014, millennials surpassed the percentage of employed baby boomers, and in the first quarter

---

8 "Cost of Raising a Child Calculator," U.S. Dept. of Agriculture, accessed January 15, 2017, https://www.cnpp.usda.gov/tools/CRC_Calculator/default.aspx.

9 The overall population growth rate hit its peak in the late 1960s and has been declining ever since. According to United Nations projections, the rate has dropped to 1.18 percent annually. Just ten years ago, it was 1.24 percent annually. Global population will continue to rise, estimated to reach about 9.7 billion people by 2050 even with the drop in fertility in the industrialized world. Most of that growth will come from just eight countries: the Democratic Republic of the Congo, Ethiopia, India, Indonesia, Nigeria, Pakistan, Tanzania, and Uganda. See also: United Nations, Department of Economic and Social Affairs, "World Population Prospects," ESA/P/WP.241, 2015, https://esa.un.org/unpd/wpp/Publications/Files/Key_Findings_WPP_2015.pdf.

of 2015 they surpassed Gen Xers to become the largest share (more than fifty-three million strong) of working Americans.[10]

This shift has remarkable impact, not simply because of the growing proportion but also because of significant differences in what millennials are looking for in the workplace. Generally speaking, this generation has not experienced anything close to the financial deprivation and economic disruption their parents and grandparents endured. While this is a significant economic accomplishment for the United States, it does highlight one of the important framing issues around jobs that is significantly different from previous generations. Simply having a job is no longer enough. Members of this generation are often characterized as seeking opportunities in which they not only make a difference but also see how their personal contributions create impact. There is nothing wrong with this mentality per se; it just highlights the different mindset of millennial job holders.

Also—thanks to parents, coaches, and changing rules for competition—as children, millennials usually received trophies just for participating or carried home seventh-place ribbons to tack on their bulletin boards. These experiences naturally increased their appetite for validation and recognition—even if it was simply for showing up. This may be why research now suggests there is a rise in narcissism in this generation,[11] which does not bode well for authentic teamwork and collaboration.

The millennial view of work is essentially different. Yes, millennials need a job to be able to afford the lifestyle they want to live, but they also want to be proud of what they do, enjoy the time they

10 Richard Fry, "Millennials Surpass Gen Xers as the Largest Generation in U.S. Labor Force," Pew Research Center, May 11, 2015, accessed March 14, 2016, http://www.pewresearch. org/fact-tank/2015/05/11/millennials-surpass-gen-xers-as-the-largest-generation-in-u-s-labor-force/.

11 For a review of recent research on this topic, see: Sadie F. Dingfelder, "Reflecting on Narcissism," *Monitor on Psychology,* February 2011, accessed January 15, 2017, http://www.apa. org/monitor/2011/02/narcissism.aspx.

spend at work, build their social networks, and be validated (even rewarded) for their involvement in work assignments, regardless of the outcome. Most organizational leaders and managers are ill-prepared to respond to these needs.

These two forces working together—a shortage of talented labor in combination with employees' preferences on when, how, and even where they work—will lead to what we refer to as the *Age of Choice*. In this Workplace 3.0 era, not only will employees have more specific demands related to their employment, they will have a multitude of choices on where to work based on a growing level of talent scarcity. While this may be seen by some as primarily a crisis of recruitment, we see it more as a crisis of leadership and managerial capacity.

The fact is, in the Age of Choice, when employees of any age cohort have a toxic manager, they will be far more likely to seek employment elsewhere. Without the fear that they won't be able to find new work, employees will not need to endure toxic managers or conditions. Instead, they will simply quit and try their chances elsewhere.

IMPACT ON LEADERSHIP

In this environment, managers need to create the conditions where people look forward to coming to work. For example, the Gallup organization, after an extensive meta-study of research around workplace engagement, estimated that about 70 percent of the factors influencing employee engagement are "owned" by managers. Toxic managers, those limited to hierarchical, punitive-based, "my way or the highway" approaches, will become expensive liabilities to their companies. As a general rule, employees *join* companies and *quit* managers.

Companies that respond early to this new labor reality will find it easier to recruit and hold onto talent, stay apace with the growing services and product appetite from existing and new clients, and remain highly competitive from a cost perspective. They will also notice that their clients, their community, and the business media will be far more likely to note the broad positive implications of their high-performance culture.

Organizations slow to recognize and adapt to these coming changes are going to be at a distinct competitive disadvantage. They will have higher rates of turnover, higher costs for training (and retraining), recruitment challenges, higher labor costs (since the primary way they will be able to attract and retain talent will be through signing bonuses and higher salaries), and lower levels of workplace engagement. It will also be harder to build and maintain high degrees of customer engagement.

The most efficient solution to this new labor reality is for organizational leaders and their management teams to adopt science-based, empirically validated strategies and actions. The strategies laid out in this book are designed to create the conditions where we know employees can thrive, where they will perform at a level much closer to their full capability.

This book can correct decades of outdated management practices and help stem the hemorrhaging of talent and profits resulting from ineffective leadership. You can help remove the barriers to extraordinary workplace cultures with insights and tools that allow employees to "thrive by design."

There are many great leadership books in print that deal primarily with individual elements of the workplace ecosystem (teams, leader character, trust, etc.), but few (if any) of them trace back to the neurological origins, let alone the behavioral underpinnings, of why employees change their performance in pro-employer directions. This book does.

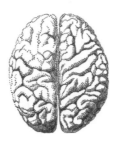

CHAPTER INSIGHTS

➔ The Industrial Revolution kicked off the *Age of Compliance*, a time when employees were just grateful to have a job to support their family, and managers could easily lead with a "my way or the highway" approach.

➔ As we move into the *Age of Choice*, we face two competing dynamics, a growing need for highly skilled talent at the same time the rate of labor growth is in decline. This means there will be fewer highly skilled people available to fill new and existing jobs in a growing economy.

➔ Millennials are now the largest segment of the professional workforce. Rather than searching for job security alone, they seek opportunities where they can make a difference and see their personal contributions make an impact—and they are not afraid to change jobs until they find them.

➔ Toxic managers don't create the conditions where employees look forward to coming to work. In the Age of Choice, these leaders face increased turnover and decreased team engagement, performance, and profitability.

CHAPTER ACTION STEPS

➤ *Reflect:* Run through a mental list of the employees that report directly to you. Do you know what drives them to show up to work every day? Have you created an environment that offers challenge, meaning, and purpose? Or do you operate with a "my way or the highway" approach?

➤ *Act:* Workplace dynamics are shifting; draft your strategy for how you can adapt your leadership style and why that matters to your organization.

➤ *For Manager Resource Center subscribers:* Visit ManagerResourceCenter.com and review the timeline found in Step Four of the Foundation section. This snapshot of workplace evolution reinforces why employee engagement is more important today than ever before.

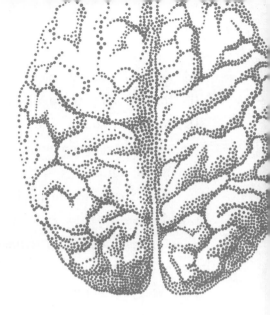

CHAPTER 2

RELATIONSHIP SCIENCE

Humans are fundamentally a social species whose social environment has shaped our genes, brains, and bodies, and our biology has fundamentally shaped the social environments we have created.[12]
— *The Oxford Handbook of Social Neuroscience*

The dominant ecology for the human being is other human beings.[13]
— Dr. James Coan

Imagine that our species, after countless centuries of trial and error, has found a "sweet spot" where we perform at our best and maximize our chances not just for survival but for success. And imagine that this knowledge has been refined and honed down to lessons so vital that they have been hardwired into the brain and passed from gener-

---

12 John T. Cacioppo and Jean Decety, "An Introduction to Social Neuroscience," in *The Oxford Handbook of Social Neuroscience*, edited by Jean Decety and John T. Cacioppo (New York: Oxford University Press, 2011), p. 3.

13 James Coan, "The Social Regulation of Emotion," in *The Oxford Handbook of Social Neuroscience*, edited by Jean Decety and John T. Cacioppo (New York: Oxford University Press, 2011), p. 618.

ation to generation as a part of our genetic heritage. Envision as well that these neurally etched principles serve as behavioral blueprints for leading a successful life and are deemed so essential for survival that they are dictated unconsciously, impacting virtually everything we do throughout our lives.

If this were true, the implications for business and public service would be remarkable. Organizations, having broken the code for what drives human action and wellness, could build workplace cultures that nurture those conditions and train leaders (at all levels) on how best to support employee performance. Imagine that building highly engaged workplace cultures were that easy!

It is.

Amid the hundreds of leadership books and millions of pages written on the subject, it turns out that nothing is more important to the success of an organization than the straightforward application of new, empirically validated outcomes from the neurosciences and clinical research on what drives our behavior at a core (in fact, cellular) level. My colleagues and I call it "thrive by design."

As a species, we share about 99.9 percent of our DNA with each other. While it's true that no two humans are perfectly identical, we are, from a genetic perspective, strikingly similar. This similarity includes a biological operating system, passed along in the human genome, that gives the brain a road map for how best to survive and prosper. The brain is still too much a mystery to have total clarity on the *why* behind everything we do—but there is exciting evidence that offers a new level of understanding on practical leadership approaches for organizations.

Embedded in our genome (and the approximately twenty thousand genes it harbors) is a shared hunger to have social connection. Human beings, it turns out, are herd animals, hardwired all the way down to the cellular level to have safe and secure connections with others. These *others* help ensure our survival by scanning for mutual threats, sharing the workload, and helping to defend against predators (among countless other benefits). There is, in short, a tremendous advantage to having social resources, and the brain thrives when it knows they are available.

When we have these neural nutriments, life feels better; when we don't have them, we wither. This need transcends differences in gender, education, generation, and ethnicity, giving leaders and human resource professionals new means to impact all employees. I find it interesting that while a substantial part of the leadership literature stresses our differences (personality types, behavioral, decision-making styles, etc.), what turns out to be much more important is what we have in common—the need for safe and secure connections. The need to avoid social isolation (referred to later in this book as *emotional isolation*) is universal and ubiquitous—it affects all human beings whether at home or at work. This hunger for connection, a prosocial frame that surrounds everything we feel, think, and do, has what neuroscientists call *control precedence* in the brain. It is not simply a goal or objective—it's a behavioral imperative.

I FIND IT INTERESTING THAT WHILE A SUBSTANTIAL PART OF THE LEADERSHIP LITERATURE STRESSES OUR DIFFERENCES (PERSONALITY TYPES, BEHAVIORAL, DECISION-MAKING STYLES, ETC.), WHAT TURNS OUT TO BE MUCH MORE IMPORTANT IS WHAT WE HAVE IN COMMON—THE NEED FOR SAFE AND SECURE CONNECTIONS.

The fight, flight, or freeze response isn't just for the impending attack of a predator; it is also there to protect us from the imminent danger of relationship threats, social isolation, and communal condemnation. Because of this need for connection, the mere thought of being isolated can be triggering even while surrounded by others. "Humans . . . fare poorly both mentally and physically, especially when they *perceive* they are socially isolated."[14] In other words, it isn't being ensconced in the crowd that delivers the neural nutriment, it is the felt experience of safe and secure connections that are real and readily available.

While I said earlier that these needs are universal, I recognize that some people feel their needs are different. Often managers in our workshops offer what they see as exceptions. "I don't feel that is true for me," one manager told me. "I just see the need for employees to step up and get the job done like I would do." These encounters with contrarians and doubters led me to ask myself, "If the need for social resources is so essential, why isn't it more obvious in our thinking?"

Research sheds light on why some people feel that our stance on isolation doesn't apply to them. We are only aware of what rises to our consciousness, so if we do not have specific thoughts or musings about needing social connection, it makes sense that we might believe this innate reality isn't "true for me." The fact is, most of what we do in life happens without having specific conscious thoughts that trigger it.[15] Researchers explain that it would be difficult to survive if we actively pondered every single step and decision, so our sur-

---

14 Cacioppo and Decety, "Introduction to Social Neuroscience," p. 5.

15 Neuroscientists point out that most of the cognitive, affective, and behavioral processes governing our actions occur unconsciously, with only a subset of the end products reaching awareness (Timothy Wilson and Yoav Bar-Anan, "The Unseen Mind," *Science* 321, no. 5892 (2008): 1046, doi: 10.1126/science.1163029). See also, Kahneman, Daniel. *Thinking, fast and slow.* Macmillan, 2011.

vival-tested brain does most of the heavy lifting in the background. Humans have an "adaptive unconscious that allows people to size up the world extremely quickly, make decisions, and set goals—all while their conscious minds are otherwise occupied."[16] Just because we don't sit around consciously worried about our relationships with friends, family, and colleagues doesn't mean the need for them isn't driving our actions. An iceberg is a good metaphor; at the surface level you only see the top 10 percent, while 90 percent of the floating mass of ice lies unseen below the surface. Just below the surface of our conscious thoughts lies the subliminal mass of incontrovertible and unconscious behavioral intention—the need to belong, to be valued, and to have social resources in times of need.

Historically, human beings evolved in close-knit social groups, clans, and tribes. Our ability to endure the rigors of life was dependent on trust, hyper-cooperation, and our ability to work together in predictive and consistent ways. If you were alone on the open savanna of East Africa, for example, your chances of surviving were very small, and that is why there was a singular advantage to being in a group. Whether individuals used the clan to distribute workloads or for defense, the default imperative in the brain was to get into a group where you were valued, able to contribute, and could trust at least some of the others to watch your back.

In a paper from Cambridge University,[17] researchers use sophisticated statistical analysis to look for "ultra conserved words" that have existed since the end of the last Ice Age. Of the twenty-three words representing so-called "deep language," ten of them are overtly relational. Words like "thou," "we," "who," "ye," "mother," "to give,"

---

16 Ibid.

17 Mark Pagel, Quentin D. Atkinson, Andreea S. Calude, and Andrew Meade, "Ultraconserved Words Point to Deep Language Ancestry Across Eurasia." *PNAS* 110, no. 21: 8471–8476 (2013), doi: 10.1073/pnas.1218726110.

and "to hear" demonstrate the deep relational roots of our human history.

Today we are all progeny of individuals who figured out how to cooperate, how to work with others to overcome the often brutal realities of life in early societies. Obviously, most of us don't grow up in close-knit tribes anymore, but there is a modern-day proxy—the workplace. When you ask the question "Where do we spend most of our time while awake with other adults?" the answer is clear—at work. In a very real sense, one could argue that we are *hardwired* to go to work—to gather with others, to work toward common goals, and to maintain perhaps our most meaningful social community.

The implication that work is the new tribe is a significant one for leaders, if only from the perspective of how to lead more effective teams and improve individual performance. In ten years we will look back and celebrate those business leaders who learned how to better integrate the latest science regarding human behavior into the workplace. More on how to do this follows in subsequent chapters, but before we examine what can be done, we need to better understand the science behind *why* the actions we suggest work so consistently and effectively.

THE BIG PICTURE

We've learned more about the brain in the last ten years than we have in the previous thousand. Recent advancements in *where* things happen—assigning regions of the brain to specific tasks and body functions—have been matched by valuable insights into *why* things happen behaviorally.

The brain is much more than a neural computer working in isolation, which is how researchers framed it for much of the twentieth century. The historic tendency of scientific inquiry to focus on the smallest scale possible (i.e., individual cells, singular traits, parts per billion) makes investigational sense, but it has left out the larger, comprehensive, and systemic purpose and objectives of the whole person.

If you had all the parts of an automobile distributed to individual investigators, for example, would their detailed analysis of just one component apiece help you understand the physics of locomotion? The ease of analysis from a small unit perspective is obvious, but such a perspective can easily cause us to overlook the big picture. Fortunately, new research in social neuroscience, adult attachment, and prosocial behavior is shedding new light on what compels our behavior—not just by looking at differentiated psychological processes, but by capturing the organizing principle of the whole person as well.

In these pages, I have attempted to move published, peer-reviewed scientific insight into actionable leadership strategies. With a focus on creating high-performance workplace cultures, we now look at two congruent areas of research that deliver the greatest insight into how organizations (social groups) impact individual performance.

SOCIAL BASELINE THEORY

A brilliant neuroscientist and clinical psychologist, Dr. James Coan of the University of Virginia, was trying to find the neural mechanism or gate that reduced felt pain when someone is in the presence of a close friend or partner. He had an ingenious setup for the experiment. Female volunteers would lay down in an fMRI (functional magnetic resonance imaging) scanner to map the tiny metabolic changes that take place in the active parts of the brain (a safe and noninvasive technique). He attached electrodes to their ankles that would be used to deliver a small electric shock randomly during the experiment (painful for sure, but not dangerous). He did the research in three stages, first with a trusted partner holding the woman's hand, then with a stranger holding her hand, and finally with the woman by herself. The results were startling, with the self-reported and measured levels of pain increasing at each stage. The volunteers experienced the least amount of pain with a loved one (what researchers refer to as a safe and secure attachment figure), more pain with a stranger, and the maximum discomfort when alone.

Coan searched in vain for the neural mechanism that reduced the pain. In months of sifting through the data, he and his team could not find the means by which the brain was interrupting and reducing the pain the volunteers felt when they were in the presence of a trusted partner. Then it hit them—what if the process they were observing wasn't the result of the pain being *reduced* in the presence of the attachment figure? What if, instead, the baseline for the way the brain registered pain was to assume the presence of social resources, with the pain *increasing* as those resources were diminished, first with the stranger (less predictable) and finally while alone (no social resources, total isolation)?

This is, in fact, the conclusion he reached and published. He named this model of brain functioning *social baseline theory* (SBT) to underscore the game-changing clarity that the brain not only functions more effectively in a prosocial environment, but it assumes it is in one already. The shorthand version is this: we are hardwired at birth to have safe and secure connections with others. This is how our species not only survived across the centuries but also excelled at the top of the food chain and intellectual hierarchy. This social resources-rich orientation continues today, deeply seared into virtually every fold and crevice of the brain.

Coan's SBT model of brain functioning suggests that having available social resources sets the most efficient metabolic cost for the tasks we face throughout the day because, Coan writes, "the brain construes social resources as bioenergetic resources, much like oxygen or glucose. . . . To the human brain, social and metabolic resources are treated almost interchangeably."[18] In other words, the human brain, in its evaluation of how costly tasks will be (and wanting to perform at the highest level of efficiency), sees social resources (other people) as metabolic energy. This means the effort required to accomplish tasks can be distributed to others in the group (work team, department), and that in turn reduces the individual's perceived burden for doing the work.

> The social baseline model of emotion regulation . . . suggests that social proximity and interaction are not *only* strategies for emotion regulation, but also that they are the primary, default, or *baseline* emotion regulation strategies employed by many social species, not least humans. This is in part because social proximity and interaction is fundamental to human ecology, much as water is fundamental to aquatic species. That is, in contrast to specific climates, diets, landforms, or other obvious environmental characteristics, the dominant ecology for the human being is other human beings.[19]

---

18 James A. Coan and David A. Sbarra, "Social Baseline Theory: The Social Regulation of Risk and Effort," *Current Opinion in Psychology*, February 2015, 1:87–91, doi: 10.1016/j.copsyc.2014.12.021.

19 Coan, "Social Regulation of Emotion," p. 618.

Conversely, when this baseline expectation of available social resources is violated, the brain functions less effectively, primarily as a result of increased acute and chronic distress. As I will elaborate later in the book, this explains why disengaged employees (who typically exhibit lower levels of trust and reliability) are so corrosive to the behaviors of others on the team. Interestingly, this phenomenon can also explain why many workers become so disengaged. When employees come to work every day in environments that are punitive, hierarchical, and unpredictable (just to name a few negative conditions), it makes perfect sense that they would slide toward disengagement because these conditions are so counter to what our brains need and look for every day.

The cost of not having helpful resources goes well beyond the workplace.

> Social proximity and interaction are essential components of human health and well-being. Over the past decades, a tremendous amount of research has documented that strong social relationships, access to rich social networks, high perceived social support, and positive social development correspond with measures such as decreased basal cortisol, decreased autonomic reactivity, decreased susceptibility to illness, more rapid recovery from wounds, decreased vulnerability to mental illness, and even extended longevity.[20]

Other behavioral researchers have made similar findings under a different label—what they call *prosocial behavior*—reporting a con-

---

20 Ibid., p. 620.

nection between those individuals exhibiting prosocial behavior and a multitude of benefits.[21]

> Cultivating friendly relationships among members of one's own local community pays . . . when it comes to emergency aid (survival). . . . Forging long-term friendly alliances assures us that we have someone to call when we need something. A recluse cannot rely on others and accordingly bears a steep cost. The degree to which one is approachable and a reliable reciprocator predicts the degree to which one is sought out as a candidate in the reciprocity pool. There are long-term benefits to being nice, and cultivating a positive reputation with other group members plays a critical role in gleaning benefits.[22]

This is precisely why it is vital for organizational leaders to create and sustain workplace cultures that support and encourage employee engagement. This isn't about tactics for making employees *happy* (the focus of many engagement programs); it is rather about creating *alignment* of the workplace to the hardwired expectations and needs of the brain, thus allowing individuals to perform at their best, full capacity. Sadly, the "action plans" developed by many leaders to increase their employee engagement scores miss the mark in this regard.[23]

---

21 For a helpful compendium of prosocial research, see: Laura M. Padilla-Walker and Gustavo Carlo, eds., *Prosocial Development: A Multidimensional Approach* (New York: Oxford University Press, 2014).

22 Patricia H. Hawley, "Evolution, Prosocial Behavior, and Altruism: A Roadmap for Understanding Where the Proximate Meets the Ultimate," in *Prosocial Development: A Multidimensional Approach,* edited by Laura M. Padilla-Walker and Gustavo Carlo (New York: Oxford University Press, 2014), p. 59.

23 For more background on how to more effectively measure employee engagement, see chapter 9.

There is one more piece of research I would like to review that corroborates Coan's social baseline model. This research examines task accomplishment more directly. Dr. Dennis Proffitt of the University of Virginia (UVA) and colleagues from several other universities conducted a very revealing study where they asked individuals and, separately, paired friends to put on a heavy backpack and then assess the steepness of a hill on the UVA campus. The participants were randomly selected as they were out walking, having no previous knowledge of the research. The friend pairs (tested for the strength of their friendship) were considered to have high levels of social support during the experiment, and those participants who were walking alone when selected were considered to have low levels of social support. The outcome? Participants who were with friends saw the hill as less steep, and the longer the friendship, the lower the hill's incline. The researchers then replicated the study at Plymouth University in England, only this time each participant was alone and was asked to imagine one of three acquaintance types:

1. Someone of great personal importance who made them feel good and who would provide help in a difficult situation (characterizing positive support)

2. Someone they saw frequently but did not know personally and whom they neither liked nor disliked (neutral support)

3. Someone who was once important to them but who betrayed them or disappointed them in a time of need (negative support)

After focusing on one of the three relationship types, each participant was escorted to a hill (similar in steepness to the hill in the first study at UVA) and was asked to assess the incline. The results were consistent with the first study, with participants who thought of the positive social resource estimating the hill to be less steep than those participants who thought of a neutral or negative contact. The "closeness and warmth associated with the imaged other mediated perception of hill slant. . . . The more positively participants felt toward their imaged contacts, the less steep the hill appeared to them."[24]

These are two of many examples where trusted social resources increase the capacity and endurance of those who either have them in immediate proximity or who simply imagine them. The opportunity here for organizations and their leaders is not only obvious, it is essential to the ability of every employee to reach their full capacity and potential when at work. There are multiple impacts for employees: their state of mind, their physical well-being, and the volume of work they can reasonably accomplish. This process of load-sharing will be discussed in more detail in the next chapter.

ATTACHMENT THEORY

While Coan's social baseline model points out how those who socialized in clans, groups, and tribes had significantly higher rates of survival (and efficiency with tasks), the late Dr. John Bowlby's studies on attachment, dating back to World War II, have shown us the debilitating effects of isolation. More recently, the remarkable research around adult attachment conducted by Dr. Susan Johnson in conjunction with Coan removes any ambiguity on the neurological benefits of safe and secure connections,[25] and pioneering work

---

24 Simone Schnall, Kent D. Harber, and Dennis R. Proffitt, "Social Support and the Perception of Geographical Slant," *Journal of Experimental Social Psychology* 44, no. 5 (2008): 1246–1255, doi: 10.1016/j.jesp.2008.04.011.

25 S.M. Johnson, M. Burgess Moser, L. Beckes, A. Smith, T. Dalgleish, R. Halchuk, K. Hasselmo, P.S. Greenman, Z. Merali, and J.A. Coan, "Soothing the threatened brain: Leveraging contact comfort with Emotionally Focused Therapy," *PLOS ONE* 8, no. 11 (2013): e79314.

by researchers Dr. Phil Shaver and Dr. Mario Mikulincer on the role of adult attachment in organizations may rank among the most important (and undervalued) developments in the field of human resources in decades.

Bowlby was a British doctor who aided British soldiers during World War II suffering from what was then called "shell shock."[26] Today, we know the condition as post-traumatic stress disorder (PTSD). At the same time that Bowlby was doing his work, caregivers in another part of Great Britain were taking care of war orphans. These solitary children, each the only survivor of their family, were being cared for in foundling homes (orphanages). Unfortunately, many of the children in these homes were dying, and the doctors couldn't stop the deaths because they had no idea what was causing them. These homes were clean and warm, and regular, nutritious meals were served. On paper, these orphans should not be dying.

When the doctors in these homes came across Bowlby's work, they realized that the symptoms he was describing in shell-shocked soldiers were similar to those the orphaned children suffered from.

OUR HUMAN NERVOUS SYSTEMS ARE WIRED FOR CONNECTION WITH ONE ANOTHER AND WHEN WE DON'T GET CONNECTION, ESPECIALLY IN A MOMENT OF NEED, THE BODY SUFFERS.

Bowlby was asked for his expertise, and as a scientist, he approached the issue very rationally. He gathered the data, analyzed it, and made a discovery: if we are left alone to deal with hardship, we won't cope well. His conclusion, decades before neuroscientists would corroborate it, was that our human nervous systems are wired for connection with one another and that when

---

26 John Bowlby, *Attachment and Loss, Vol. 1: Attachment* (New York: Basic Books, 1969).

we don't get connection, especially in a moment of need, the body and the heart suffers. We are distressed, we hurt, and, as his research highlights, some of us die.

If we do have those connections, we can endure almost anything, because we can rely on those relationships to get comfort and soothing, to repair and refuel. Bowlby's conclusion? We find and build our resilience through connecting with others, especially during stressful times.

The science behind adult attachment clearly establishes that without safe and secure relationships, we become "emotionally isolated." Being disconnected from others (personally or professionally) takes a toll. Emotional isolation is devastating to the human nervous system. As Bowlby discovered, isolation is inherently traumatizing. The percentage of Americans who say they are isolated has doubled since the 1980s from 20 to 40 percent. Emotional isolation disrupts sleep patterns, increases stress hormones, and raises the risk of stroke by 32 percent and heart disease by 29 percent.[27] It has been labeled a public health hazard, and the magazine *Psychology Today* referred to it as a "modern plague."[28] A pervasive sense of being alone and isolated with no hope can actually trigger the immune system to stop doing its work.[29] "The magnitude of risk associated with social isolation is comparable with that of cigarette smoking and other major biomedical and psychosocial risk factors," according to researchers.[30]

---

27 Dhruv Khullar, "How Social Isolation Is Killing Us," *New York Times,* January 4, 2007, accessed March 29, 2017, https://www.nytimes.com/2016/12/22/upshot/how-social-isolation-is-killing-us.html.

28 Stephen Ilardi, "Social Isolation: A Modern Plague," *Psychology Today,* posted July 1, 2009, accessed March 29, 2017, https://www.psychologytoday.com/blog/the-depression-cure/200907/social-isolation-modern-plague.

29 Janice K. Kiecolt-Glaser, Phillip T. Marucha, William B. Malarkey, Ana M. Mercado, and Ronald Glaser, "Slowing of Wound Healing by Psychological Stress," *Lancet* 346, no. 8984 (1995): 1194–1196.

30 James S. House, "Social Isolation Kills, But How and Why?" *Psychosomatic Medicine* 63, no. 2 (2001): 273–274.

But more importantly, as Bowlby discovered decades ago, emotional isolation can be deadly, and that's why the war orphans were dying.

EXTENDING ATTACHMENT THEORY INTO PROFESSIONAL RELATIONSHIPS

Attachment theory holds critical answers to human vulnerability throughout our lives. With its primary goals of protection and security, whether at home or at the office, seeking and maintaining contact with a secure relationship "is viewed as the primary motivating principle in human beings and an innate survival mechanism."[31] Threats—real or perceived—activate the attachment system, which drives one toward a protective figure such as a boss, leader, or parent. Seeking reassurance, clarity, direction, and protection, safe attachments help individuals cope with threats and maintain focus. Once a threat is mitigated, the individual can return to the task at hand. If the threat isn't mitigated, the individual remains preoccupied; loses focus, clarity, and creativity; and stops taking appropriate risks (thus showing less initiative).

As Coan and other researchers have discovered more recently, Bowlby saw our need to seek comfort and protection from attachment figures as a biologically hardwired response, integral to survival and productivity. This helps us understand, for example, the intense bonding that often happens among troops in combat, the bonding that happens between colleagues who have successfully completed a project, the bonding among team members in sports, as well as the bonding that happens in healthy romantic relationships.[32]

---

31 John Bowlby, *A Secure Base: Parent-Child Attachment and Healthy Human Development* (New York: Basic Books, 1988).

32 Sue Johnson, *Love Sense: The Revolutionary New Science of Romantic Relationships* (Little, Brown and Company, December 31, 2013).

The Gallup Organization has a survey that includes the question "Do you have a best friend at work?"[33] While people don't actually need *best friends* at work, they do need trusted colleagues; they need at least one safe and secure attachment on the job. In fact, Gallup's exhaustive research has shown that if someone does have at least one trusted relationship with someone in the office (what they call "vital friends"), that employee is up to seven times more engaged when they get to work.[34]

While Bowlby's original work was primarily around children and their caregivers, more recently his work has been extended into the role of adult attachment in the workplace. The workplace is the new tribe, and the attachments that adults are innately seeking, those safe and secure connections, are frequently made with the other adults they interact with at work. The research on adult attachment in the workplace indicates that employees will use their relationship with a group as a safe haven (a source of support and comfort) and as a secure foundation for growth and exploration. This process is enhanced by the cohesiveness of the group, which increases an employee's ability to learn and improves their team performance. Two of the leading researchers in this area sum it up this way: "The higher the group's cohesiveness, the more its typical members feel protected, comforted, supported, and encouraged by the group."[35] This in turn improves employee engagement, loyalty, and commitment.

The same benefits occur when organizational leaders develop effective relationships with staff. "Effective leaders are likely to be

---

33 "The Gallup Q12 Index," accessed February 6, 2017, http://www.goalbusters.net/uploads/2/2/0/4/22040464/gallup_q12.pdf.

34 Tom Rath, *Vital Friends: The People You Can't Afford to Live Without* (New York: Gallup Press, 2006).

35 Mario Mikulincer and Phillip R. Shaver, "Applications of Attachment Theory and Research in Group and Organizational Settings," in *Attachment in Adulthood: Structure, Dynamics, and Change* (New York: Guilford Press, 2007), p. 434.

available, sensitive, and responsive to their followers' needs; provide advice, guidance, and emotional and instrumental resources to group members; develop followers' autonomy, initiative, and creativity; build followers' sense of self-worth, competence, and mastery; support their desire to take on new challenges and acquire new skills; affirm their ability to deal with challenges; admire and applaud their successes; and encourage their personal growth."[36] These conditions, when offered in consistent and predictable ways, allow employees to thrive. The connections we make at work, especially with our leaders, can provide a secure foundation and a safe haven that enhances an employee's ability to function closer to their full capacity.

Attachment is a moderator of sorts. When things aren't going well in the organization, there is less resilience if social bonds are tenuous or mercurial. When the members of a team have good working relationships (safe and secure connections), more gets done at a lower metabolic cost to individuals and at a lower financial cost to the company. Employees feel less taxed (their perception of the slope declines), and they are able to get more accomplished. By having those connections, people are better able to deal with any sources of angst or anxiety that arise throughout the day.

Sometimes employees form their strongest connection, even at a distance, with a key leader in the organization, typically with a dynamic and relational CEO or president. Some employees attach in an even broader sense with the mission and vision of the company. When employees establish a link between their personal calling and the mission and vision of the company, the organization itself, as the embodiment of that purpose-giving action, can become a source of attachment. I have found this to be particularly true in my work with health care organizations. Nurses, who work in what

36 Ibid., p. 440.

can be a challenging environment (on several levels), talk about the mission of helping patients as their primary motivation, helping to offset the typical sources of disengagement, especially regarding self-perceptions of being underpaid. In one health care company, when we asked employees why they like working there, one of the most prolific responses was "because we are helping save lives." This mission-focused factor compensates for many of the more pernicious conditions they may endure at work.

The value of creating and sustaining a workplace with trusted and reliable (safe and secure) social resources is undervalued in contemporary management and leadership literature. The more cursory approaches advocate the need to create "cool" and exciting organizational cultures as a way of increasing a company's curb appeal. This approach pales in comparison to the profusion of benefits released when employees feel safe and connected at work. The more connections that can be created, nurtured, and supported, the stronger the bond with the employee, and that in turn results in more engagement. Since the beginning of the Industrial Revolution, the design of the workplace has almost exclusively been around process, procedure, and production. It's time to move up to the next level, where forward-thinking leaders at all levels in the company are focused on relationships, connections, and emotional well-being.

The importance of emotional connection has even permeated the automobile industry. At the 2017 Consumer Electronics Show in Las Vegas, Honda showcased a concept car that can understand the driver's emotions and create its own emotions in response. At the core of this development is a form of artificial intelligence, which Honda refers to as an "emotion engine," that will allow machines to create their own emotions artificially. In a rare example of how attachment theory translates into the world of high tech, Honda says the automobile will be able to have conversations with the driver to gauge their emotions. The stated goal is to evoke feelings in the driver that the car "has become a good partner and thus form a stronger emotional attachment toward it."[37]

There is more than a little irony in the business focus over the last several decades on efficiency initiatives like Six Sigma and getting "lean," when in fact the largest underutilized resource in organizations is the human brain. Don't get me wrong—I'm fully in support of business process improvement programs. It's just that the most valuable source of business improvement can be found in how we train our leaders to connect and engage with the most important assets in the company—its employees. If organizational leaders spent as much time on why 70 percent of their employees are disengaged as they do on squeezing an additional 1 percent improvement out of processes and systems, they would discover the source of double-digit improvements in productivity, profitability, and reduced turnover, just to name a few.

When leaders ignore these immutable laws of human performance, the costs are high. Turnover is one of the biggest challenges companies face today. The number one reason why employees quit, according to the *Harvard Business Review*, is a bad relationship with their immediate supervisor or boss.[38] It's clear that toxic, unsafe relationships have a harmful impact on the person as well as the organization. More of the harmful costs of disengagement (and how to turn that around to reap the bounty of true employee engagement) will be discussed later in the book.

---

37 Steven Overly, "This Honda Concept Car Will Have Emotions of Its Own," *Washington Post,* December 8, 2016.

38 "Why People Quit Their Jobs," *Harvard Business Review,* September 2016.

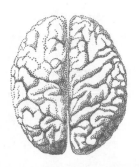

CHAPTER INSIGHTS

↪ Regardless of gender, education, generation, or ethnicity, our brains all require safe and secure connections in order to truly thrive. When we have these strong connections, we thrive. When we don't, we wither.

↪ Our species evolved and survived through the generations by sticking together in clans, groups, and tribes. We are hardwired to be in groups for mutual support, safety, and survival. Today, we spend most of our time while awake with those we work with—which means that in the twenty-first century, *work is the new tribe.*

↪ Coan's *social baseline theory* indicates that our brains assume they are in a safe and secure environment with a wealth of social resources and support. If we lose those valued resources, the mental and emotional cost is powerful and debilitating.

↪ It is vital that leaders create alignment between the conditions the brain seeks every day (reliable social resources) and the daily experience of employees.

Doing so allows employees to function closer to their full capacity.

↪ Bowlby's *attachment theory* indicates that our nervous systems are wired for connection to one another. When those connections are severed, we can feel emotionally isolated and our bodies suffer. Connections are also important in the workplace; employees are more likely to thrive when they have trusted social resources at work.

↪ Rather than following the trend of creating "cool" workplace environments (which can shift from year to year), leaders who focus instead on a relational culture where employees connect with core values, organizational leaders, mission and vision, and each other will benefit from a more sustainable and healthy work environment. As the quality of connections increases in the work culture, so do the levels of engagement.

CHAPTER ACTION STEPS

↪ *Reflect:* How can you foster an environment where your team members can connect with one another, you, and the organization's mission and vision?

↪ *Act:* Talk to each of your team members in your next one-on-one to help them understand how their work makes a difference to you, the team, and the company. Draw clear connections between their efforts and team or organizational goals.

→ *For Manager Resource Center subscribers:* Visit ManagerResourceCenter.com and take the **Building Trust Self-Assessment** found in your Toolkit section. Use your score to gain insights around how you create trusting relationships with others at work.

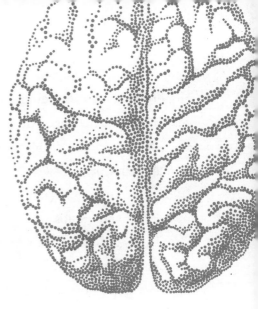

C H A P T E R 3

LIMBIC GOVERNANCE

*"Across social species, individual members do not
fare well when living solitary lives."*[39]

*"Our brains are not solitary information processing devices any
more than the cell phone is a solitary information processing
device. The cell phone has been designed to connect to other
cell phones, and its very existence and function depends on
connection with other such devices. Our brains have evolved to
connect to other minds, and our remarkable accomplishments
as a species reflect our collective ability, as instantiated in
each individual brain, rather than our individual might."*[40]

—The Oxford Handbook of Social Neuroscience

We are a thriving species because we have learned to pool and share
social resources. This is as true today as it was in tribes in the ancient

---

39 John T. Cacioppo and Jean Decety, "An Introduction to Social Neuroscience," in *The Oxford Handbook of Social Neuroscience*, edited by Jean Decety and John T. Cacioppo (New York: Oxford University Press, 2011), p. 5.

40 Ibid, p. 7.

past. We may be surrounded by modernity (glass skyscrapers, the cloud, and instant communication), but to the brain's limbic system, the world hasn't changed much. The "limbic brain" (our shorthand for referring to the limbic system and its precedence in shaping human behavior) still sees the world through a relational lens that prioritizes our actions and thoughts through interactions between individuals and groups.

This is a different paradigm from how most of us have viewed the brain. The brain isn't just a sponge for learning, and it serves a far more important and complex service than processing information and overseeing motor function. It also guides us with thousands of silent voices—a steady stream of neural messages urging us in a direction the brain *knows* will increase our success and well-being. This wiring has been with us since birth. When the brain finds itself in an environment where specific desirable conditions exist, it thrives. A primary objective for leaders at all levels is to encourage a felt sense of safety so the hyper-attentive and hyper-vigilant functions of the brain can stand down.

THE LIMBIC BRAIN

In a remarkable book, *The Archaeology of Mind: Neuroevolutionary Origins of Human Emotions,* authors Jaak Panksepp and Lucy Biven highlight the different functions of two key parts of the brain: one new, one old.

> The neocortex is an organ that generates complex cognitive abilities as well as culture, and it is definitely important for complex perceptions, learning, and cognitions. The neocortex is responsible for almost all of the cultural milestones that human beings have been able to achieve. . . .

However, the cortex could achieve nothing without an evolved foundational mind deeper in the brain. . . . Our most powerful emotional feelings—the primal emotional affects—arise from ancient neural networks situated in the brain regions below the neocortical "thinking-cap." . . . It is "archaeological treasure," for it contains the sources of some of our most powerful feelings. Those ancient sub-cortical brain systems are precious, multi-hued "jewels" for anyone wishing to understand the roots of all the basic values we have ever known and will experience in our lives.[41]

When it comes to typical explorations of employee engagement and what drives it, virtually all of the research has been at a cognitive level: trying to understand the *types* of behaviors cataloged as pro-engagement (relatively easy to witness and measure) and the *sources* or *triggers* of those beneficial behaviors (rather difficult to detect and measure). In contrast, researchers in both social and affective neuro-science encourage us to dig deeper into the mind to find answers on why certain workplace conditions may represent a more anciently rooted origin of exemplary behavior.

Although neuroscientists have long known much about the ancient emotional circuits of our brains, these circuits have only recently been definitively linked to our emotional feelings. This allows neuroscientists to delve deeply into the neural substrates of affects—the menagerie of our basic internally generated feelings. Which brain systems bring us joy? Why are we sometimes sad? . . . How do we

41 Jaak Panksepp and Lucy Biven, *The Archaeology of Mind: Neuroevolutionary Origins of Human Emotions* (New York: Norton, 2012), pp. ix–x.

experience enthusiasm? . . . The traditional behavioral and cognitive sciences cannot provide satisfactory answers to such profound issues.[42]

There is more to this point. The authors highlight that "in many ways, the neocortex—the source of our human intellect—is the servant of our emotional systems." In effect, emotion "impels the neocortex to find ways of meeting our needs and desires" and "to do things that make us feel important and in command of our destinies. . . . Mankind's great and unique achievements, the products of our prodigious neocortices, are firmly rooted in the psychic energy provided by this system."

The limbic system, in the midbrain, includes the subcortical systems that oversee our emotional lives and is an important player in what we learn and commit to memory. It helps us make sense of the world, particularly in terms of our emotional experience and our *felt sense* of being safe or unsafe. What leaders need to know about the limbic system is, first, that it has control precedence in the brain (it can override other brain functions when triggered), and second, that the limbic system has no idea whether it's at work or at home. Stated more plainly, emotions cannot be removed from the workplace, and they certainly should not be ignored.

The amygdala is a small almond-shaped structure that is a key part of the limbic system, helping us determine whether we feel happy, sad, or scared. Psychologists would say the limbic system, and the amygdala in particular, helps us assess the emotional valence of situations—essentially determining whether the situation is positive (happy, calm) or negative (angry, fearful). It also is involved in storing memories and learning connected to punishment and reward. Emo-

---

42 Ibid., pp. 5–6.

tionally loaded memories, which are more likely to be recalled later, are consolidated with the help of the amygdala and its seahorse-shaped neighbor, the hippocampus (considered to be critical in forming new memories). Most leaders reading this understand how important these capacities for learning, retention, and positivity are in maintaining a highly engaged workforce.

The limbic system is an emotional processing supercomputer (faster, actually). It's also the heart and soul of the fight, flight, or freeze mechanism. It's constantly vigilant for things that could be harmful. It's not very exact or deliberate in its assessment of danger; rather, it tends to make snap judgments that assume and exaggerate threats that may not be real. Researchers say it "favors false positives." Let me explain.

Imagine yourself walking through a field with grass about twelve inches tall. As you walk from point A to point B, in your peripheral vision you pick up an object that's narrow, black, and about three feet long. Immediately your limbic system sounds the alarm. "Snake!" echoes in your brain and your body might freeze, recoil, or prepare to defend itself. In reality, it's actually just a branch that's fallen out of a tree. In this example, the branch is a false positive—that is, it isn't a true threat. The job of the limbic brain is to assume there's danger even when there isn't any. Why? So that we won't be caught off guard, unprepared, and less able to defend ourselves. This offers a distinct advantage (survival bias), apparently, over those brains—now long extinct—that were missing this function. Therefore, we are all descendants of Homo sapiens who were—in addition to being hyper-cooperative—hyper-vigilant threat exaggerators.

We see this play out in the workplace every day as employees assume the worst when their manager ignores them (the manager was actually just preoccupied) or they are "excluded" from an "important" meeting (the manager just didn't want to waste the employee's time), or after a particularly pointed feedback conversation (where they might assume they are about to get fired). Every leader in the organization needs to be more attuned to these powerful drivers of emotional regulation. Once triggered, they are metabolically exhausting distractions, resulting in everything from more workplace accidents to increased health problems.

I was struggling to come up with some visual imagery to help managers in our workshops grasp and remember the key takeaway about the limbic brain—that it's not very discerning and is hyper-attentive to any possible danger. One of the easiest ways to help people understand something is to help them visualize it—whereas words are abstract to the brain, images are tangible and real. Once, at a conference, a researcher told me that members of his team jokingly talk about the limbic brain in relation to a certain animal. "It's not very smart and it is hyper-attentive to danger," he said, "just like a squirrel." We have embraced the squirrel metaphor in our work, and our clients love the imagery. It helps convey the limbic system's hyper-attention to danger: "Better safe than sorry."

The limbic system is responsible for threat detection, and it often exaggerates danger just to be on the safe side. At E3, we love this picture of a squirrel—not very bright but hyper-vigilant for threats, real and imagined.

Dr. James Coan lightheartedly says the limbic system (the squirrel) is asking two questions all day long: "What's next?" and "How am I doing?"[43] These two questions, broad generalizations drawn from his own research and observation and dozens of other studies about brain function, are remarkably helpful for leaders looking for actionable models to improve workplace engagement.

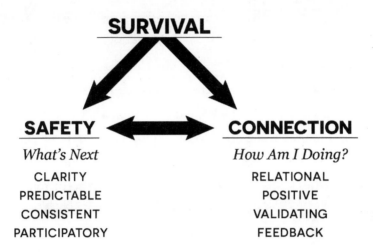

SURVIVAL

SAFETY ⟷ **CONNECTION**

What's Next | *How Am I Doing?*

CLARITY | RELATIONAL
PREDICTABLE | POSITIVE
CONSISTENT | VALIDATING
PARTICIPATORY | FEEDBACK

Survival is imperative for the limbic system, and leaders can gain actionable insights by focusing on two central questions the limbic system asks all day long: "What's next?" and "How am I doing?" These questions offer managers a wealth of opportunities to connect and engage with staff in pro-limbic ways.

Let's look more closely at these two questions our inner squirrel is asking all day long: "What's next?" and "How am I doing?" Ask yourself: If you don't know what's coming next, do you feel more safe or less safe? Most people would say they would feel less safe. Leaders need to answer this question more effectively for their employees. Whenever managers become more predictable, consistent, and transparent, they provide clarity on what will happen next. Whenever leaders seek closer alignment around core values, mission, and vision,

---

43 Personal conversations and conference presentations from 2007 to 2016.

they are creating a consistent and predictable culture with immediate limbic benefits.

The question of *How am I doing?* stems from our biological operating system that includes the encoded need to be in a group. Naturally, since the group's social resources are so essential for our survival, the limbic brain is constantly assessing our membership status. "Am I in?" it asks. "Do they see me? Am I valued? Do they perceive me as a worthy and unique contributor?" The limbic system doesn't ask this question occasionally; it asks the question every minute of every day.

Here, too, effective leaders can answer this question for their employees with predictability and consistency. When a manager validates and gives recognition to an employee, it's not just a gratuitous social gesture. He or she is talking directly to the limbic system; the message carries limbic resonance—"You've been noticed. You are seen and valued by one of the leaders of the tribe. You're safe, carry on."

Let's take a deeper dive into the reasonable inferences based on this neuroscience research.

1. Since the limbic system has control precedence in the brain, it is a logical source of interest among leaders who want a deeper and more effectual understanding of employee behavior.

2. The limbic system plays a primary role in determining whether we feel safe or at risk, and it sees safety through a relational lens. When we have safe and available social resources, it feels more secure, and threat vigilance (and its associated metabolic load) diminishes. In turn, our mental and physical capacity increases. This also explains, as covered in the previous chapter, why Homo sapiens are

herd animals, finding the most likely path to survival and success only when working together.

3. This brain-based model for impacting the daily experience and behavior of employees carries a powerful benefit. It cuts through much of the maneuvering associated with trying to match HR initiatives with imagined distinctions based on ethnicity, culture, gender, education, or generational cohort. I'm not suggesting there aren't differences among and within these categories—I am suggesting that there are highly effective leadership interventions that work universally among them.

4. There are thousands of tactical recommendations made in the prolific leadership books and websites published today. Of all of them, the only kind of guidance that sustainably works is the kind directly and inextricably linked to the quality of workplace relationships. The emotional connections that employees forge with company attributes such as mission, clients, colleagues, or service delivery is paramount. This also explains why so much of the leadership advice circulating in blogs and websites is anecdotal at best and often misguided. What we read on the surface may obscure the true nucleus of what, underneath, is really driving the prosocial, pro-company, and productive behavior leaders so desperately need to grow and prosper.

METABOLIC LOAD AT WORK

As mentioned previously, a key role of the limbic system is to appraise security or insecurity around available social resources, and it cannot distinguish whether we are at work or at home. So the notion that at work we become unfeeling cogs in the apparatus of the workplace, impervious to the emotional maelstroms that exist in organizations, is—to put it bluntly—delusional. The brain needs to feel safe wherever it is, and that's where a huge part of our metabolic load, the energy consumed in the brain, is dedicated—determining and getting to a condition of safety. A critical part of this felt sense of safety, social neuroscientists tell us, is to have trusted relationships.

> Human beings are social creatures at our core, and the hard-wired need to have safe and secure connections is as fundamental to our health as food and water. . . . This need for social connection goes beyond the physical proximity of others (strangers are less beneficial than family) and it includes the mere perception of being alone.[44]

According to the research of Coan and others, a key reason we are prosocial as a species is the brain's penchant for conserving the limited energy available at any given moment. The brain is essentially starved for energy; what is available has to be conserved and used for the most essential functions. Our cerebral matter occupies about 2 percent of our body mass, but it consumes 20–25 percent of our resources. There is no extra energy floating around in the soft nervous tissue packed into our skull. Everything we do, we do for a reason, and the brain is trying to conserve as much energy as possible in the trillion-plus chemical and electrical transactions made every second

---

44   Jean Decety and John T. Cacioppo, eds., *The Oxford Handbook of Social Neuroscience* (New York: Oxford University Press, 2011).

to get us through our day. According to Coan, our brain uses trusted social resources to "economize its activity."

This is the neuroscience of employee engagement. When workplace cultures nurture the conditions where human beings thrive (i.e., predictable and consistent availability of social resources), where the members of the tribe can safely load-share with one another, leaders will see remarkable shifts in daily behavior that translate directly to the bottom line. This also reveals the key driver of employee disengagement, namely an overt scarcity of trusted connections, unclear expectations, poor direction, and a high-pressure or punitive boss. Coan explains it this way:

WHEN WORKPLACE CULTURES NURTURE THE CONDITIONS WHERE HUMAN BEINGS THRIVE, WHERE THE MEMBERS OF THE TRIBE CAN SAFELY LOAD-SHARE WITH ONE ANOTHER, LEADERS WILL SEE REMARKABLE SHIFTS IN DAILY BEHAVIOR THAT TRANSLATE DIRECTLY TO THE BOTTOM LINE.

> [S]ocial resources alter perception-action links associated with intervening in the environment, such that there is less perceived alarm when perceived social resources are high, which corresponds in turn to fewer actions needed to meet demands associated with the stressor. This . . . conserves metabolically costly operations in the prefrontal cortex and elsewhere, either by simply conserving neural resources or freeing them to be devoted to other problems, thus increasing

the efficiency of coping with a potentially dangerous and uncertain world.[45]

Our neural benefits are not obtained by simply being in the presence of just anyone; we need *trusted* connections: "The performance of stressful tasks is associated with less negative affect in the presence of familiar friends than with strangers."[46] The implications of this for the workplace are monumental. Employees come to work every day with a hyper-vigilant subconscious threat assessment system that is designed not simply to detect danger but to appraise, seek, and connect with safe and secure colleagues in order to engage and thrive. When the limbic system perceives danger (such as in unclear directives and expectations, a punitive environment, or a mercurial manager), it hijacks metabolic resources that would otherwise be available for mental reasoning, task focus, innovation, and problem solving. In short, when employees don't feel safe, they have less mental acuity and capacity to do exemplary work. Employees feel more exhausted, burnout is more likely and acute, and productivity drops along with essential workplace norms like collaboration, help seeking, and relationship building.

This negative neural static is like white noise, only instead of being soothing, it is caustic and distracting. It occurs in virtually all organizations, and the bigger the organization, the more pervasive it becomes.

---

45 James A. Coan, "The Social Regulation of Emotion," in *The Oxford Handbook of Social Neuroscience,* edited by Jean Decety and John T. Cacioppo (New York: Oxford University Press, 2011), p. 620.

46 Ibid.

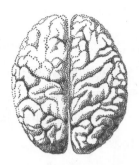

CHAPTER INSIGHTS

➡ The limbic system, which is always on the lookout for danger, has control precedence in the brain. It overrides other brain functions when our fight, flight, or freeze switch is triggered. It also doesn't differentiate between work and home life, so there is no way to separate emotions (or the need for mental and emotional safety) from the workplace.

➡ The brain is asking two questions all day long: "What's next?" and "How am I doing?" Leaders can answer "What's next?" through clear, transparent communication and by being predictable and consistent in their actions. They can answer "How am I doing?" through positive, regular interactions of validation, recognition, and feedback.

➡ When we have trusted relationships, our brains are more efficient and mental capacity increases, enabling employees to be more creative, innovative, and productive in the workplace.

CHAPTER ACTION STEPS

➤ *Reflect:* To maximize clarity, have I identified measurable targets for my team and individual employees? Is each of my employees clear on what those measurable targets are? Have I taken the time to discuss the organization's targets with my team?

➤ *Act:* Strong leaders are fully present with their staff as often as possible. Find ways to build personal relationships with each team member as you interact with them during the workday to increase their felt sense of safety with you as their leader.

➤ *For Manager Resource Center subscribers:* Visit ManagerResourceCenter.com and download **Answering Two Critical Questions** from your toolkit. This document ensures you are providing your employees with the information they need to feel safe and supported.

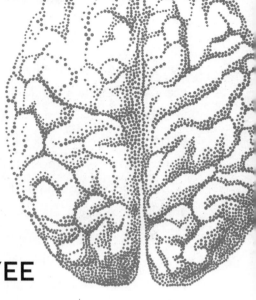

CHAPTER 4

WHAT IS EMPLOYEE ENGAGEMENT?

Fear is a bad custodian of that which is intended to last;
whereas mildness and goodwill ensure fidelity forever.[47]
— CICERO

Every employee comes to work with a choice about the level of effort they will contribute. There is a minimum amount of vigor they need to demonstrate so that management or peers don't pull them aside and ask them, "What's wrong with you today?" Every employee knows this baseline degree of labor and service that is expected of them, and they try to achieve it—at least while being observed. This base level of effort, the bare minimum, is what we would refer to as disengagement in the workplace, and in most organizations it ranges anywhere from 40 to 65 percent of employees.[48]

From that rock bottom, the sky's the limit, as employees can exercise their engagement all the way up to their full capacity as a

---

47   J. R. Stone, *The Routledge Dictionary of Latin Quotations* (New York: Routledge, 2005), p. 275.

48   Based on the global data collected by E3 Solutions in our twenty-six question online survey taken by employees (typically annually) in our client companies.

human being. How much discretionary effort they volunteer is up to them. When it happens, leaders typically refer to it as "going above and beyond" and "exceeding expectations." Some organizations attempt to bribe employees for this level of discretionary effort (some forms of pay-for-performance, for example), but such compensation schemes are insufficient to sustainably maintain employees at or anywhere near their full capacity.[49]

Engaged employees consistently volunteer their discretionary effort. This is in fact one of the most valuable benefits of a high-performance workplace, where a majority of employees are freely giving exemplary effort in their daily work. Research involving more than seven million employees globally shows firms with the highest engagement scores have a revenue stream on average 4.5 times higher than those with the lowest scores.[50]

A key objective for leaders in Workplace 3.0 is to create the conditions that trigger discretionary effort, which includes enhanced focus, deeper connection, and increased energy and mental capacity. In one paper, researchers point out that discretionary effort isn't simply *more of the same* type of effort but rather includes "innovative behaviors, demonstrations of initiative, proactively seeking opportunities to contribute, and going beyond what is, within specific frames of reference, typically expected or required."[51]

The first researcher to use *engagement* to describe the differences in employee behavior was Boston University professor, Dr. William A. Kahn. His work was published in the prestigious

---

49 See Alfie Kohn, *Punished by Rewards: The Trouble with Gold Stars, Incentive Plans, A's, Praise, and Other Bribes* (New York: Houghton Mifflin, 1999).

50 Hywel Roberts, "Engagement adds to the bottom line, research finds," HR, accessed March 26, 2017, http://www.hrmagazine.co.uk/article-details/engagement-adds-to-the-bottom-line-research-finds.

51 William H. Macey and Benjamin Schneider, "The Meaning of Employee Engagement," *Industrial and Organizational Psychology* 1, no. 1 (2008): 15.

Academy of Management Journal in 1990. At the time, most human resource specialists and organizational leaders were focused on how to get employees more *motivated* and *involved* in their work; it was a top-down approach, focused on what tactics leaders needed to use to get employees to *think* differently about their work. Kahn offered a more nuanced perspective focused on how employees *feel* about their work. His research suggested leaders needed to think "more deeply about the choices that individuals make, consciously and not, about how much of their personal selves they wish to bring in and express" while at work. He was intrigued by the word *engagement*, both because it represented the deep sense of commitment we experience before marriage and because it refers to the mechanics of connection, "to engage the clutch of a car to power an engine—which also appealed to me as a guiding metaphor about how people brought their energies into their work."[52]

Kahn felt that the results were too generalized; they were too distant from the actual psychological processes driving behavior in the workplace. He didn't like the typical research approach that conceptualized and measured worker conduct in a manner suggesting "that organization members strike and hold enduring stances (committed, involved, alienated), as if posing in still photographs."[53]

Kahn's guiding assumption was that employees are constantly making choices about how much of themselves to bring in or to leave out of their daily tasks. He was right. His seminal paper was remarkably prescient of the emerging neuroscience that highlights how our brain constantly calibrates our actions, including workplace engage-

---

52 David Zinger, "William Kahn: Q&A with the Founding Father of Engagement (Part 1)," Halogen TalentSpace, posted January 23, 2017, accessed February 18, 2017, http://www.halogensoftware.com/blog/william-kahn-qa-with-the-founding-father-of-engagement-part-1.

53 William A. Kahn, "Psychological Conditions of Personal Engagement and Disengagement at Work," *Academy of Management Journal* 33, no. 4 (1990): 693.

ment, based on the hardwired hyper-vigilance around emotional safety (i.e., predictability, recognition, empowerment) and abundant social resources (i.e., trusted relationships, effective leaders).

Employee engagement is a mindset that encourages employees to volunteer discretionary effort, resulting in improved task performance, team integration, and personal well-being. Tactics based on more cognitive (and under-theorized) approaches like employee satisfaction (notably different from employee engagement), or singular strategies focused on incentives, pay-for-performance, Employee of the Month, and the like, will never deliver the rich and robust results that come from truly engaging employees on an emotional level. I'm not saying these common tactics won't deliver results, but I do see them as pedestrian compared to aligning organizational efforts more closely to proven neural needs so fundamental that they have contoured the very structure of the human brain.

How have we missed this essential truth regarding critical drivers of human behavior? By thinking too small. As mentioned earlier, the scientific process favors precision, so there is a natural bias to look at small units; they are easier to measure, monitor, and make sense of. But the finely honed purpose of the human brain cannot be understood by looking at cell function and ganglia alone. To understand the grand scheme of what Homo sapiens need to thrive, small units won't suffice.

What does all this mean to today's business leaders? They need to embrace a broader perspective of what drives outstanding workplace conduct. Leaders at every level of the organization need a big-picture understanding of the unchanging human need for essential social nutrients. When this vital nourishment is available in the workplace, employees respond in remarkable ways. In Kahn's view, when employees are engaged at work, it results in increased "effort, flow, mindfulness, and intrinsic motivation . . . [and] . . . what researchers refer to as creativity, . . . authenticity, nondefensive communication, playfulness, and ethical behavior." In addition, Kahn found that these employees brought more "personal presence (physical, cognitive, and emotional)" to the workplace.[54]

His insights are congruent with what we see in the fields of prosocial human behavior, social baseline theory, social neuroscience, and adult attachment. Stepping back from the silos and the one-off studies used so frequently to strategize employee engagement initiatives, leaders should instead embrace the cumulative evidence from multiple scientific disciplines telling us, in essence, that the way people feel determines how they behave.

STEPPING BACK FROM THE SILOS AND THE ONE-OFF STUDIES USED SO FREQUENTLY TO STRATEGIZE EMPLOYEE ENGAGEMENT INITIATIVES, LEADERS SHOULD INSTEAD EMBRACE THE CUMULATIVE EVIDENCE FROM MULTIPLE SCIENTIFIC DISCIPLINES TELLING US, IN ESSENCE, THAT THE WAY PEOPLE FEEL DETERMINES HOW THEY BEHAVE.

TAPPING INTO ENGAGEMENT

In one sense, the neural equation regarding exemplary conduct is fairly straightforward. When the limbic system senses conditions it identifies as safe, available metabolic resources increase, resulting in better focus, more risk taking, increased creativity, and prosocial conduct. When conditions are perceived as unsafe (inconsistent and

54 Ibid., 700.

unpredictable social resources, punitive, bullying, or shaming actions from peers and leaders, etc.), the chemical processes that respond to threats take precedence and can devastate mental capacity for work-related tasks.

The paramount question for leaders is "What makes an employee feel safe?" First and foremost, the limbic system determines safety through a relational lens. "Do I have trusted colleagues (reliable social resources) at work? Are these resources available to me and safe to work with (predictable, consistent, positive, nonpunitive)? Do I find meaning and purpose in my work? Am I able to use my strengths? Do I find congruence between my values and those of my employer? Am I challenged so that I can showcase my special skill set?"

Just looking at the results of our own work measuring employee engagement in client companies, I can say that key conditions of a safe environment include predictability, consistency, fairness, recognition, and secure connections with others. Organizational leaders need to look more holistically at the constellation of popular leadership buzzwords like "trust," "incentives," "empowerment," "risk," "influence," etc., if only to get a better grasp of the *reason* these words are important. They are all important, but looking individually at these small units of the human experience does not unravel the deeper context and meaning of why these words trigger limbic resonance. Words in the brain are complex; they have to be translated into what they mean relationally, how they make us feel.

Our Western culture gives predominance to words, data, and endless analytics. Our brain, on the other hand, gives predominance to relationships and emotion (feelings). Leaders need to focus on how to do a better job of balancing and blending the two. For centuries this was the key to human survival—knowing whether to stand apart from a newcomer, to sprint to safety, or to approach them as a new, potentially valuable, social connection. This need for interconnection isn't just a social convenience; for centuries it was the difference between life and death. The reason you are reading this book today is that your forerunners were hyper-vigilant *and* hyper-cooperative.

Tribal instincts are innate for our species, but we don't grow up in tribes anymore. Or do we? The closest approximation is the workplace, the contemporary setting where we spend most of our time while awake with other adults. The excessive demands (i.e., long hours, weekend work) of today's workplace means that many employees spend more time at work than they do at home with family. A foundational tenet of our practice at E3 Solutions is that the social ecosystem we are immersed in while at work represents the new tribe for twenty-first century humans. The good news for business leaders? Human beings are hardwired to go to work, to be a part of a social ecosystem. The bad news? Most workplace environments don't deliver the conditions the brain hungers for and needs in order to thrive.

What the brain expects to find in its tribe is the ability to load-share with other people who behave with consistency, predictability, and a sense of fairness and positivity in their actions as they strive collaboratively for their collective success. Employees want to be challenged so that they can demonstrate their specific skills, and they look for strong leaders who provide clarity on mission, vision, and direction in addition to providing validation, recognition, and constructive feedback. In this environment, employees can nurture safe and secure relationships and more easily find meaning and purpose.

Most employees experience a shortfall in virtually every one of the conditions described. They might find a few of the conditions occurring occasionally, and some even report to outstanding managers who compensate for organizational or senior leadership shortcomings. But for most employees, the work environment is in some degree toxic every day. Employees in the Age of Compliance (which I described in chapter 1), with very few employment choices, had to come to work. Organizations didn't have to care about the felt experience of workers—they showed up regardless. In the talent-constrained period we are in today (and ever hereafter), employers will have to be more responsive to innate human needs, moving beyond perks and posters to key emotional drivers and true workplace engagement.

Companies that begin to view mental resources the same way they see production resources are often appalled at the waste occurring inside their organization. When an environment is noxious, the brain is naturally distracted from the goals of the organization and daily tasks—focusing instead on trying to make sense, fix, or simply avoid the toxicity confronting it. According to Kahn:

> Personal disengagement . . . is the simultaneous withdrawal and defense of a person's preferred self in behaviors that promote a lack of connections, physical, cognitive, and emotional absence, and passive, incomplete role performances. . . . [The disengaged] hide true identity, thoughts, and feelings [and uncouple] . . . self from role; people's behaviors display an evacuation or suppression of their expressive and energetic selves. . . . They act as custodians rather than innovators. They become physically uninvolved in tasks, cognitively unvigilant, and emotionally disconnected from others in ways that hide what they think and feel, their creativity, their beliefs and values, and their personal connections to others.[55]

---

55 Ibid., 701–702.

Conversely, in a safe haven environment, the brain has fewer taxing distractions, worries about basic needs are diminished, and increased mental acuity is applied to the task at hand. People become more innovative and more creative, their cognition expands, they think and act in more varied ways, and their resiliency improves when dealing with roadblocks. This is why it is so important to eliminate the *limbic* distractions to the tasks that companies expect their employees to do. Creating a safe haven environment can deliver immediate and tangible results.

This is one of the key reasons I describe an emerging "mindset economy" where employers will need to focus on sources of mental acuity as much as they do on process analysis and data collection.

A safe haven workplace is not a coddling zone where employees are pampered and indulged. Accountability, for example, is essential (as I will elaborate on in chapter 8). There are many steps that leaders at all levels in the organization can take that will contribute to a safe haven environment (see subsequent chapters on Accountability; Validation, Recognition, and Feedback; and Positive Leadership). Contrary to what pop culture says about leadership, it isn't about a specific approach, formula, or perk. There are, however, some basics that will be compulsory. All of the following are essential contributors to human thriving:

- ✓ abundant, reliable social resources (i.e., trusted colleagues)

- ✓ consistency and predictability (especially from people and processes)

- ✓ meaning and purpose (we are hardwired to be a part of something important)

- ✓ validation, recognition, and constructive feedback ("Do you see me?" "How am I valued?")

☑ fairness (impartial and just treatment without favoritism or discrimination)

☑ great leaders who make sure all these things happen for every member of the tribe

Any time CEOs and organizational leaders can support these conditions inside the workplace, employees respond viscerally— not because of what they have been *told* in town hall meetings and employee newsletters but because of how they *feel*.

Perhaps the most important outcome or benefit is that employees are able to perform (live and work) at levels closer to their full capacity. This isn't about brawn, endurance, or throughput; this is about feeling like we are operating within reach of our human design specs. This is, in fact, the origin of this book's title, what I refer to as "thrive by design," something we focus on constantly at E3 Solutions. More than a list of desirable work behaviors (see below), it is the emotional condition (and ensuing mindset) that enhances our sense of self and self-worth, gives our life meaning and purpose, and expands our performance capacity and mastery over life's innumerable challenges. We smile more, love more, feel better, form more reliable connections, and live longer. Work, not home, is the most likely place for all these conditions to exist for the twenty-first century worker, assuming organizational leaders sense and grasp the opportunity.

ENGAGED BEHAVIORS		DISENGAGED BEHAVIORS
Accountable	vs.	Blames
Solution focused	vs.	Problem focused
Shows professionalism	vs.	Gossips
Transparent	vs.	Deceptive
Loses track of time	vs.	Clock-watcher
Always learning	vs.	Apathetic
Punctual	vs.	Arrives late/leaves early

Exceeds expectations	vs.	Does the bare minimum
Energetic	vs.	Tired or lazy
Truthful	vs.	Dishonest
Consistent	vs.	Inconsistent
Proactive	vs.	Procrastinates
Communicates regularly	vs.	Lacks openness, uncommunicative
Acts with integrity	vs.	Surfs the web and social media
Empowered	vs.	"Victim"
Appreciates	vs.	Criticizes
Positive disposition	vs.	Negative affect
"Can-do" attitude	vs.	"Not in my job description" attitude
Detail-oriented	vs.	Unfocused
"We" focused	vs.	"Me" focused
Visible	vs.	Absent
Passionate	vs.	Indifferent
Resilient, adaptable	vs.	Resistant
Thoughtful appearance	vs.	Sloppy appearance
Speaks up, contributes	vs.	Silent
Volunteers	vs.	Disappears
Innovative	vs.	Lacks creativity
Inspired	vs.	Disillusioned
Focused	vs.	Distracted, forgetful
Inspires	vs.	Toxic, contagious, infects others
Persistent	vs.	Gives up easily
Proactive	vs.	Indifferent, apathetic
Relational	vs.	Transactional
Feels the "Why"	vs.	Knows the "What"
Connected with peers, leaders, and the company	vs.	Distant, lacks emotional connection

In our workshops we ask managers to describe the typical behaviors of disengaged employees. The right-hand column is a sampling of what managers tell us. We also ask for descriptions of the engaged or "A" players and a correlated list is provided in the left column.

The most successful management paradigm of the future is going to be less about pay-for-performance, organizational structure, and business strategy and far more about the daily felt experience of people when they come to work every day.

GETTING STARTED

As leaders contemplate "What should I do to engage my employees?" they need to move away from the mindset of "If I do *this*, then I will get *that* in return." Increasing employee engagement is not a barter system where managers can simply exchange "casual dress" days for a 2 percent improvement in staff productivity, for example. This is an all-too-common approach for companies focused on employee *satisfaction* (an attitude that can change at a moment's notice) rather than staff *engagement* (a predictable pattern of behavior).

Leaders should also avoid the slippery slope of trying to make employees happier. Perks are nice, to be sure, but they risk becoming entitlements that do less to increase commitment to the work than they do to embed a mindset of "What else can the company do for me?" When leaders get the right strategy in place based on relational science, satisfaction is achieved as an *outcome*, not a *precursor*. Here is my point: When employees are thriving, they feel happy as a result. In contrast, if you make someone happy in the moment (with a joke, a compliment, a perk), that does not in itself create workplace engagement. Standing alone, perks are mere palliatives, potentially masking deeper issues rather than resolving them. Company perks can be a part of a larger, more integrated approach that looks at critical elements of organizational culture such as: leader skill sets and behaviors, organizational processes and procedures, employee professional and career development, positivity, multivariate forms of recognition, and reliable feedback, among others.

We are often asked by senior leaders, "Where should I begin?" My answer is always, "With science, not leadership fads." In almost every area of business—finance, manufacturing, supply chain, accounting, etc.—companies are at the cutting edge of science. They have the best tools, equipment, software, and technology. When it comes to human behavior, however, most organizations are at least a decade behind the science. The notion that employees are lucky to have a job and that they should just do what they are told is still prevalent among leaders and managers.

The second recommendation I give is to start by better equipping managers for the complex demands they face daily related to employee performance. Focus on managers first and employees second. For decades, leaders have assumed that the emotional state and resulting mindset of employees was irrelevant. Employees were expected to align themselves with the organization—that was part of the job, a part of what it meant to be on the payroll. When employees didn't perform well, leaders assumed it was the fault of the workers. One well-known CEO of a Fortune 100 company would simply fire the bottom 10 percent of performers every year. That might seem decisive, but it isn't effective. The truth is, it's likely that the majority of people in that "bottom 10 percent" were there for reasons related to the quality of their leadership, especially the manager they reported to directly.

We find this all the time in our employee engagement evaluation survey tool, the E3A. It is common to find the majority of disengaged employees clustered under poorly equipped (in training and resources) managers. It would be ludicrous to assume that firing these employees would benefit the organization. In fact, one former employee of that Fortune 100 firm told me that the process actually "terrorized" employees because no one knew who was going to go next, and the atmosphere was one where everyone was looking around to make sure some of their peers were struggling. A better solution would have been to acknowledge that employees' workplace demeanor is heavily influenced by the conditions they experience within the microculture created by their manager. It is time to stop blaming employees and start better equipping managers with what we know will make a difference. Of course, there are employees who "arrive" disengaged and will likely underperform regardless of circumstances. Our experience is that cohort (the unmovable *actively disengaged*) represents less than 5 percent of workers.

CONCLUSION

Business leaders have been inundated with a slew of popular books and programs that lay claim to the silver bullet of employee engagement or high-performance cultures. It's not simply about trust, accountability, challenge, or personal autonomy. While results can flow from getting intentional around any one of these topics, those words are not a magic solution to engagement in and of themselves.

Much of what we have seen in working with CEOs in Great Britain and North America is a disappointment with one or another new leadership quick-fix buzzword. They jump on the bandwagon and soon lose commitment as results turn out to be ambiguous. Organizational interest then wanes and a strong appetite emerges for the next "big idea." And so the cycle of leadership marketing trudges on.

What is wrong with this approach? Well, for one, it exhausts managers and supervisors who are asked to leap from one so-called great idea to the next. The whole process also implies that business leaders need to constantly look for the latest fix rather than something far more substantial and rewarding in terms of behavioral outcomes.

The conditions that allow human beings to thrive in the workplace are remarkably consistent, and they don't require a constant shift between the business leadership flavor of the month or year.

Anything that creates limbic resonance, tapping into our emotional need for social resources, validation, and meaning, will lead to more lasting, positive outcomes. Some leaders might think it's just about making employees more productive—but that's just the icing on the cake. It's about creating a more resilient culture, a more consistent and predictable experience for customers. It's about creating a place where people look forward to coming to work because of the quality of the relationships they have and the meaning and purpose they find when they get there.

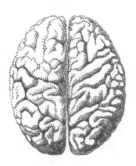

CHAPTER INSIGHTS

➡ Key managerial behaviors in a highly engaged workplace support: predictability, consistency, fairness, recognition, and secure connections with others.

➡ Employees want to be challenged and demonstrate their specific skill sets so that they can be valued, contributing members of the team. They look for strong leaders who provide clarity on mission and goals and offer consistent validation, recognition, and feedback.

→ In a safe environment, employees' cognition literally expands, so they can think and act in more innovative ways and demonstrate more resilience and initiative when facing roadblocks. When work is a safe haven, employees not only thrive—they volunteer discretionary effort every day.

CHAPTER ACTION STEPS

→ *Reflect:* Am I allowing my employees to work on tasks that are both challenging and achievable? Are they set up for success? Do I support and recognize their efforts and contributions? Do I show up in a predictable and consistent manner every day for my team? Do I offer clear, transparent communication with my team members so that they know our goals and vision?

→ *Act:* Schedule monthly one-on-one meetings with each of your staff members to explore their answers to the previous questions.

→ *For Manager Resource Center subscribers:* Visit ManagerResourceCenter.com and download **Increasing Discretionary Effort** from your toolkit. This document helps you create the conditions where employees want to give more of themselves to the work they do each day.

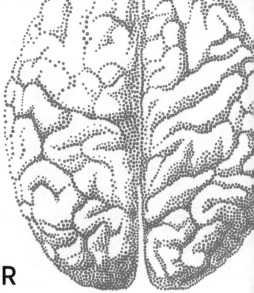

CHAPTER 5

NEW MODELS FOR CONFRONTING DISENGAGEMENT

Just as engineers need to base their work on good theories from physics, and physicians need to base their work on good theories from chemistry and biology . . . business people . . . need to base their work on good theories from the behavioral and social sciences.[56]

—C. Daniel Batson

One of the biggest human resource hurdles facing business today is getting employees engaged—and keeping them in that frame of mind and behavioral mode. One piece of good news is that it appears a state of engagement is both natural and preferred by the brain. This isn't a case where we have to work against our hardwiring. Having said that, most studies for the United States and Europe indicate that around 60–75 percent of employees are disengaged. One recent study

---

56   C. Daniel Batson, *Altruism in Humans* (New York: Oxford University Press, 2011), p. 233.

found that one out of three employees are so disengaged they would change jobs just to gain the right to adjust their office temperature.[57]

Employees' expectations of what constitutes a desirable place to work is shifting at lightning speed compared to the pace of change in management theory and practice.

The solution to this shift is to use a science-based, empirically validated approach to creating the conditions that will virtually guarantee higher levels of workplace engagement. Human performance is not simply the result of efficient processes, elegant organizational structures, or pay scales (although these are valuable influencers). Just about every process improvement scheme (lean, Six Sigma) has been applied and run their course. There is little remaining competitive advantage in deploying these strategies, and they are peripheral to what really drives human behavior.

Management theory was created around companies that were built and prospered in an era of labor abundance. There are no empirically validated management theories for success in today's workplace. Most of the management theory created and used even today was based on managing people in a routine and boring job performance environment. So while the nature of work has moved to a new level, we don't really have proven models of management that draws out the best in people. Most organizations continue to use the old hierarchical, top-down, punitive management model or they react to catchy ideas such as a flat hierarchy or aggressive pay-for-performance schemes, none of which will maximize success over the long term.

Creating workplace conditions where employees thrive is not well understood in business. That isn't because business owners and

---

57 "State of the American Workplace," Gallup.com, retrieved February 26, 2017, http://www.gallup.com/reports/199961/state-american-workplace-report-2017. aspx?g_source=WWWV7HP&g_medium=topic&g_campaign=tiles.

leaders don't want to create this environment, but because they have never had to. Where dad and granddad went to work at Sears, IBM, and Kodak and expected to stay there in a secure job for decades, millennials average less than three years in one position.[58] Millennials are also more focused on their own personal goals than generations past; they're more concerned about self-actualization and finding meaning and purpose in their work. This new mindset is something many companies don't know how to work with.

As I mentioned earlier, the demands on leaders at every level in the organization have never been more complex than they are today. It is no longer enough to simply keep people in line and stay on budget. Today's manager typically deals with a combination of quality control concerns, compliance issues, utilization rates, employee drama, absenteeism and turnover, rigorous metrics, customer demands, and little access to the leadership ranks above them when they need help.

Helping managers acquire the necessary skills to effectively navigate the terrain of Workplace 3.0 may be the most important business goal for senior leaders over the next decade. The skill deficits are enormous. For example, Gallup estimates that only one out of ten managers has the natural capacity to excel in the position, while another two have the essential abilities but need coaching and structure. The other seven out of ten managers, however, will notably struggle to perform well.[59]

Managers at all levels in today's organizations are just trying to keep their wits about them and reduce their anxiety. They're looking for tips to manage people, often because they were promoted into a managerial role but weren't given instructions on how to actually

58 "Employee Tenure Summary," Bureau of Labor Statistics, released September 22, 2016, accessed February 26, 2017, https://www.bls.gov/news.release/tenure.nr0.htm.

59 Randall Beck and Jim Harter, "Why Great Managers Are Rare," Gallup.com, posted March 25, 2015, accessed April 1, 2017, http://www.gallup.com/businessjournal/167975/why-great-managers-rare.aspx.

lead other human beings. This is a big issue. In business today, the promotion process in most organizations is no more sophisticated than assessing which of the candidates has the longest tenure.

We take people who are typically demonstrating great competence in their current position and promote them into management, effectively taking them out of their career field and mastered skill sets. In a way, many of them have effectively been elevated to a position of incompetence; they're literally moved out of their scope of expertise and into a role requiring skills more familiar to human resources (HR) professionals. This is precisely why most managers refer uncomfortable personnel issues to HR staff rather than handling it themselves; they just don't feel qualified to deal with the drama. However, the most likely locus of change for employees is with their most immediate relationships, the ones that mean the most to them. The struggling manager needs to understand that by handing off tough conversations essentially to third parties in another department (albeit highly qualified third parties), they lose a lot of their behavioral change leverage. This is exactly where the "leadership" part of their portfolio should be demonstrated.

THE ROLE OF CULTURE

The new leader paradigm has less to do with the structure of the organization and much more to do with the felt experience of the people within it. The Internet has pages and pages of parsed definitions of "corporate culture," but many of those descriptions deal only with what is on the surface, not the deeper things actually propelling employees' behavior at an emotional level.

If you want to know what your culture is, just answer this question: "What does it feel like to work here?" The answer to that question is one of the most accurate assessments of the health of the workplace and, I would argue, of your real culture. Why? Because the way people *feel* determines how they *behave*. The essential question is, do they feel safe or unsafe?

CEOs need to think of their culture as part of the overall company strategy, just like the bricks and mortar and machinery, the processes and intellectual property. Culture can influence people's daily behavior, integrity, accountability, commitment, and even their health. Knowing how to

IF YOU WANT TO KNOW WHAT YOUR CULTURE IS, JUST ANSWER THIS QUESTION: "WHAT DOES IT FEEL LIKE TO WORK HERE?"

create a more effective culture can help you achieve a broad range of things—better productivity, greater profitability, less turnover and loss of intellectual property, easier recruitment, etc. This isn't just about having a "cool" culture; it's about as bottom-line focused as you can get.

As I explained in chapter 1, we are on the cliff edge of the most severe labor shortage we've experienced in this country since World War II. It's been masked in the mists of the previous recession (and years of a historically low rate of recovery). Even in this period of economic retraction (the "Great Recession"), the rate of labor growth in the United States continued to decline. As the US economy began to recover, hiring picked up and employers noticed fewer and fewer available employees with the talent levels they required. Every time you read that job growth is increasing, also know that talent, especially in positions that require high-competency skills, is in shorter supply. In this new environment, which will be characterized more by employee scarcity than abundance, those companies and cultures that conduct business as usual are going to be at a tremendous disadvantage.

With the combination of less available talent and a growing economy, we are literally entering a phase where demand will outstrip supply. And there are only two ways to attract and retain talent in that environment. You have to either pay more to get them and keep them, which puts you at a disadvantage, or create a place people love to come to work. Every leader will need to decide which of these strategies they prefer.

GETTING IT RIGHT

People want to be part of something. People want meaning and purpose when they come to work. When they look back over the forty years of their professional career, they want to know that what they did mattered. And for many people, that goes beyond what they achieved as an individual; it's about the role they played in the tribe. Working at a company that's creating an appreciable social good helps to leverage their own contribution; they did what they could as an individual, but rather than being just a ripple in a tide pool, they were involved in something that felt like a sea change.

The workforce is no longer driven primarily by a frame of deprivation. Even though everyone doesn't have the luxury of changing jobs on a whim (yet), if the connection with their employer is tenuous, they will often move on if given the opportunity. Today, it's not about job security and building tenure; it's about finding work that is fulfilling, includes some autonomy, and has a mission, purpose, and value set that fits with the employee's own.

Leadership theory and practice needs an overhaul if organizations want to get anywhere close to workers' true capacity and performance in Workplace 3.0.

THE EVOLUTION OF LEADERSHIP

The definition of a great leader has shifted over the last several decades. Leadership initially focused on individual characteristics (roles and traits). This is a category I refer to as **Leadership 1.0**. The style of Leadership 1.0 places emphasis on the role of the leader within a workplace hierarchy, with specific regard to transactional rewards and punishment. A 1.0 Leader is primarily characterized by his or her specific traits of dominance, hierarchy, rewards, and punishment. This type of leader likes to keep their direct reports at a distance and is more focused on staff respecting their "superior" position than on the quality of employee relationships. It is a top-down model where the leader is typically punitive around mistakes rather than curious. The image of the old-school Marine drill sergeant fits this style.

The next evolution, **Leadership 2.0**, places high value on a leader's behavioral style and his or her image and vision. Leaders who are inspirational, charismatic, motivational, and who emphasize an exciting vision of the future fall into this category. However, leaders in this category still tend to be narrowly focused on immediate outcomes rather than long-term goals, and they use many control tactics familiar to 1.0 Leaders. The 2.0 Leader is more focused on relationships but still relies on hierarchy and comes across more like a disciplinarian than a trusted colleague. This type of leader may be charismatic at a distance but relationally inconsistent and at times toxic. Without naming specific individuals, there are many well-known CEOs who fit this mold.

Leadership 3.0 is more focused on whole workplace ecosystems, including the quality of social interactions necessary to create a positive, safe, and productive work environment. A 3.0 Leader is transformational, team focused, and collaborative. They see the value in small but positive interactions and are able to effectively support the strengths of their team members while identifying opportunities for improvement. The 3.0 Leader is strategic, relational, and positive and sees their role more as the lead facilitator of a positive social ecosystem than a hard-nosed taskmaster. Wall Street won't appreciate this type of leader's pro-culture, pro-employee style initially, but when employee retention and level of engagement are seen as leading indicators of company health, even the hard-nosed business analysts will come to appreciate the advantages of a highly engaged workforce.

One quick analysis of a leader's style is through the lens of inclusiveness and collaboration. Does the leader do things *to* employees or *with* employees? In those cultures and companies where things are done *with* employees, engagement is typically higher because questions essential to the limbic system like "What's next?" and "How am I doing?" are answered. Unfortunately, managers often operate in silence, making decisions behind closed minds and closed doors. Instead, it's now apparent that they should be working collaboratively with their direct reports to make more inclusive decisions.

Where things really go awry is when managers struggle in their leadership role and then employees are blamed for performance or operational failings. In many cases the manager is completely unaware that the employees' performance problems stem from a lack of effective leadership (ironically, often their own). In order for leaders to be successful in a new role they're given, they need to be given more than a new title—they need a new portfolio of skills. But the new skill set they need to excel in is not the competency they mastered in their previous position.

HOW DOES A LEADER GET PEOPLE TO FOLLOW?

As I stated earlier, most supervisors and managers are not naturally equipped to manage other adults. This is why many in managerial positions operate in such dysfunctional ways. When human beings feel overwhelmed by workplace drama, deadlines, and dilettantes, one expression therapists use is that we get "flooded." When this happens, managers lose cognitive capacity and can become more reactive. Another term to describe this situation is emotional dysregulation, which occurs when our behavior becomes more automatic and less thoughtful and our actions are guided by deeply embedded models in the brain on how to cope with stress. Often, the model we have seen leaders reach for in these moments is parenting (or a version of how they were parented in times of high stress). That's why so many managers and supervisors get hierarchical and punitive. It's the most deeply embedded model their brain can find when flooded. As you can imagine, the parental approach is typically a poor model (top-down, hierarchical, traditionally punitive around mistakes) for leading adults.

When the leader takes that "parent" role, employees tend to get pushed into a "one-down" position similar to the role of "child." Most adults obviously don't want to be treated like children, and they certainly don't want to be patronized. Consequently they become resentful and angry, and sometimes they'll react in childish ways, like getting revenge, striking back with some sort of organizational or cultural sabotage.

This does not mean employees don't want strong, effective leaders. There is a tremendous difference in how we perceive *hierarchy* and someone acting in a *hierarchical* manner. Hierarchy is the most enduring form of leadership ever created by Homo sapiens (it has survived for centuries), primarily because people like outsourcing decisions that are big in impact, scope, spending, direction, or strategy. Most people don't wake up in the morning wanting to take on the enormous metabolic loads that come from regularly making big decisions that impact the lives of others. They love having those decisions made by people they trust and have faith in; they want the comfort that comes from knowing that they and others in the tribe are in good hands. That faith is oriented toward a number of traits; sometimes people want a leader with sheer strength and determination, or a keen strategist, or someone who is empathetic and understanding (or some mix of all of these).

However, when leaders act *hierarchically*, for example telling direct reports, "I'm the boss, so we're going to do it my way," the result is usually disengaging. That stance may mandate compliance, but it doesn't encourage people to follow at the best of their ability. Most people will do what they're told, but that doesn't mean they'll look forward to coming to work every day or offer discretionary effort when they show up.

Instead of the hierarchical approach, managers should work alongside employees, acting in more of a coaching role and providing continuous, positive feedback. People want to follow a leader who makes them feel that their opinions are heard, considered, and valued. They want to feel their role is not only important but also potentially unique. Employees will follow when they feel that the label given to them by their leader is congruent with how they see themselves.

CHANGING BEHAVIORS

Managers and senior leaders need more effective approaches than just telling people what to do or how they should perform. So how do managers get people to behave differently, to change entrenched behaviors? According to research conducted by neuroscientists, you're not going to get people to really change unless you can trigger limbic resonance.

Limbic resonance is a term used in neuroscience to describe the activation of highly motivating emotions. Stated differently, people have to feel the need to change at an emotional level. For instance, let's say a woman in her fifties who has been a smoker since her teens is shown pictures of a blackened lung and had all the life expectancy statistics explained to her, but she's still smoking away because all the cognitive information doesn't shake loose her addiction. Then one day she quits cold turkey—come to find out, it's because her first granddaughter was born. The strong feelings of wanting to go to that child's high school and college graduations could certainly be an example of limbic resonance. That event created the deep-seated emotions that enabled her to overcome chemical addiction and stop smoking.

This may explain why much of the corporate training conducted today, especially around change management, doesn't really take hold. For the most part, leadership training is very cognitive and tactical, it may brilliantly display statistics and studies, but it typically fails to resonate at an emotional magnitude that imbeds the knowledge. Instead, training needs to be more closely linked to conditions the brain associates with survival (increasing felt safety) and success (more effective job skills leading to anticipated validation and recognition from leaders).

THE ROLE OF THE MANAGER ON EMPLOYEE ENGAGEMENT

While a corporation may have a great enterprise culture that leaders have worked for years to create, if an individual in the organization works in a microculture under a pernicious manager, that person is not going to feel the positive impacts of the enterprise environment. This is how managers can hijack the positive cultural attributes of an organization and do things that are really quite destructive. To be fair, the reverse is also true. An employee may work for a great manager who has created a microculture of trust, collaboration, consistency, and predictability, while the larger location subculture or enterprise is toxic. In this scenario, the manager's microculture insulates his or her team from the toxicity of the larger culture. In this case, it should be noted there is a high metabolic cost to the manager in this insulating role (it's exhausting).

The manager's role is paramount and can trump whatever it is that the organization is trying to do at the enterprise level. The key is to create congruence among the cultures, to align the various subcultures (team, department, location) with the overall enterprise culture. This contributes significantly to a safe haven environment that will support employee engagement.

One of the easiest ways to nurture a safe haven environment or a felt sense of safety for employees is to increase predictability and consistency. If employees report to a manager, for example, who is inconsistent and unpredictable, that's crazy-making for the brain, and those employees will rarely reach their full potential.

Inconsistency doesn't always come from a manager. It can also come from other aspects of the organization. Working in a punitive, hostile environment will prevent people from thriving. Threats, loud voices, shouting, anger, and disruption can also serve to undermine a safe haven environment. Now note: safe haven also relates to culture, and the definition of culture is contextual. For instance, in certain industries, it might not be uncommon for people to use profanity throughout the day and still feel perfectly safe there. But in many organizations, and most office environments, that kind of language would be perceived as hostile; it wouldn't create a place where people feel safe.

Employees benefit from strong attachments with their peers, manager, and leaders and with the mission and vision of the organization. But at the end of the day, it is managers who must create the conditions where people look forward to coming to work, and when they accomplish this, their employees will outperform others in the organization who don't have those safe and secure attachments (social resources). The concept of safe and secure attachments is synonymous with a felt sense of safety and the efficient use of mental energy (more accurately, metabolic capacity). When the brain has safe and secure attachments, then the finite resources of the brain can be dedicated to more productive work-related tasks.

In addition to consistency and alignment, a vital aspect of engagement is how (and how often) employees receive recognition and validation. Direct supervisors play a critical role in acknowledging exemplary work habits because they are the ones in leadership positions who tend to be closer and have more daily contact with the rank-and-file employees. As providers of validation, recognition, and feedback, their role can be more direct and have more impact than senior leaders in the organization. Members of the senior leadership team tend to be focused on the strategic aspects of the business; they're not actively, intentionally supervising individuals, since much of their attention is rightfully focused on creating strategic direction, a healthy culture, and (hopefully) consistently expressed core values.

It is typically the person in the most immediate supervisory role who actually has the greatest face-to-face opportunities to send daily or regular messages to employees around how the organization values what they are doing. But their beneficial role in this regard has become more difficult as they get overwhelmed by their reporting responsibilities: metrics, increasing data complexity, utilization rates, etc. The more time they spend with these cognitive tasks, the less they can impact how people feel and perform when they get to work. If employees have a supervisor who is good with numbers but not with the relational aspects, they're typically going to be less engaged. If they have a manager who is all relational but can't manage numbers, they'll feel less secure. Without a balance, higher levels of employee engagement will prove elusive.

THE COST OF THE DISENGAGED

Now, there is a certain class of employees who just don't care about how they show up. They're angry. They feel like victims. They're grudge collectors. They view management and the company as a whole as being against them. It's very difficult to reach those employees and shift their behavior. Most of the time, employees act negatively because something in their brain feels threatened. For some employees, this is baggage they bring with them to the organization; they bring a history of being threatened and intimidated by previous employers or past experiences. When people feel undervalued, unsafe, or at risk, they use coping strategies such as anger and antipathy. And some employees have been so conditioned to negative experiences in the workplace—real or perceived—that they bring high levels of anger, indifference, and a "not in my job description" attitude with them every day.

What does disengagement look like? If you were to look for it in your workplace, what would you discover? Likely you'd see people showing up late or chronically calling in sick, with low productivity and a general lack of focus and negative or even toxic attitudes.

One CEO reported to me that the disengaged employees actually "hijacked his culture"—the legacy he was creating was being stolen from him by the company's disengaged employees. This highlights one of the major costs of disengagement—senior leaders become discouraged. When the founder, owner, or CEO gets discouraged and starts pulling away from the business and the goals of the company, the energy and positive inertia is corroded. As a great preacher once told me, "If there's a mist in the pulpit, there's a fog in the pews." When the leader's vision is obscured by the negativity of the disengaged, the entire company can suffer.

That discouragement can trickle down to other members of the senior leadership team. When senior leaders get discouraged, they can be distracted from implementing the goals, objectives, and strategy of the organization. The behaviors of the disengaged can distract senior leaders functionally (loss of productivity), intellectually (loss of focus), and emotionally (loss of desire or commitment). In addition, the behaviors of the disengaged erode the credibility of leaders. Other members of the organization, for example, will question how serious management is about core values when toxic employees are allowed to stay.

In addition to behavioral costs—the stress and anxiety that metabolically exhausts managers (and staff) at the end of the day—there are hard dollar costs as well (i.e., scrap, redos, returns, lost customers, turnover, etc.). When our clients begin monetizing the costs of disengagement, they are often stunned.

The damage done to company reputations can also be costly. With today's technology, a disgruntled employee can vent online before he or she even exits the premises. Have you checked your company's online ratings? You might be surprised what people are saying about you on websites such as LinkedIn, Vault, Indeed, and Glassdoor. There are even smartphone apps where employees can vent anonymously about their employers, and no cease-and-desist order can end the tirades—tirades, by the way, that are now protected as "free speech" rights and can become a permanent digital assault on a company's reputation.

While a company's leader or HR rep can reach out and respond to negative comments online, nothing inoculates against bad reviews like an organization full of engaged employees. Healthy workplaces encourage employees who care about the company. When they learn of inaccurate information, they'll defend the organization— a valuable asset against disgruntled and disengaged workers who weren't the best fit for your culture in the first place. The best way to avoid the negativity in the first place, is to build and nurture a high-performance culture.

Granted, potential customers or employees surfing the web for information on your company might be able to identify a hothead by their comments, but when those comments multiply, they can really stack up against your brand. Customers, vendors, and potential job applicants frequently review these sites to help them assess a potential relationship with your company. Customers want to review others' experience with your brand, and vendors don't want to taint their own reputation through association (especially if the claims against you include abuse of employees, sexual harassment, discrimination, or other major offenses). Potential new hires want to get a look at how current employees feel and to get a sense of the culture they might be joining. Turning off any of these stakeholders can be very expensive.

The deeper you get into a company's org chart, the more likely you are to find low levels of employee engagement. Interestingly, those employees who are paid the least and get the least amount of attention are often the ones who have the most face time with the customer. These are the employees working the retail counter, the tellers at the bank, the drivers for a service or distribution company. These are the people who spend the most time with the customer, and yet these same employees are typically given the least amount of attention, validation, and support to help them foster those important customer relationships.

GUIDE THE CAPABLE, RELEASE THE DISENGAGED

Fortunately, most of the somewhat disengaged employees[60] can, with more effective leaders, be guided into better workplace habits, attitudes, and performance. This entire book is devoted to encouraging leaders to do just that, with empirically validated and theorized approaches that invariably work . . . well, almost invariably. Unfortunately, some employees will never engage and ultimately need to be dismissed. They are almost always in the category my company calls the *actively disengaged*. When their performance doesn't shift despite intervention, there is a point of no return. When it becomes clear that an employee isn't capable of shifting to more engaged behaviors, they should be released to the market as soon as possible—hopefully to nest with a competitor!

One of the most convincing reasons why the disengaged need to be released is their disproportionate impact on the look and feel

---

60 For a complete description of the four levels of employee engagement refer to Chapter 9 and the bell curve on page 177.

of the social fabric inside the company. Now imagine, if you will, a company with an equal number of actively engaged and actively disengaged employees. You might think that this represents a balance in the organization. It might seem that the positive, high-energy people would neutralize the impacts of the disengaged ones. However, our experience in the field shows us that the actively disengaged have a disproportionate impact on a company's culture, even if there is a higher percentage of actively engaged employees. The reason this happens may be best explained with an example.

Jane is an actively engaged manager at Globex Corporation, and John is an actively disengaged manager. At work, they're civil to each other and generally like one another. But John is a grudge collector and sees himself as a victim, and one day he goes into Jane's office and starts talking about everything senior management is "doing" to him. Jane, like most of us, is a conflict avoider, so all she really wants is for John to leave her office. As they stand there with John venting, Jane nods her head in acknowledgment of his story, which John misconstrues as agreement.

If you were to ask Jane about the conversation after the fact, she would deny any endorsement of John's negative views, feeling she was neutral on the matter. But if you asked John, he would say he left Jane's office feeling validated. "No question," he would say, "she agreed with everything I said." This is how the actively disengaged can march forward thinking others align with their point of view. The disengaged can have a disproportionate impact on the culture in large part because the actively engaged tend to stand down when confronted with disengaged colleagues. Engaged employees, including managers, need better skills in protecting the company culture by holding the naysayers accountable. We offer an approach for this very process in chapter 8, on accountability.

Disengaged managers can be even more damaging than employees at the ground level. The time to give up on a manager is when they're aware that their behavior is a big slice of the problem but they just don't care. Willingness to change would be the number-one reason for continuing to invest in this kind of manager. If they aren't willing to change, it's not worth the organization's time and resources. Few organizations have the resources to coach and mentor a recalcitrant manager to the point of redemption. And it should be noted that the longer leadership waits to dismiss these employees in managerial roles, the harder it will be to find equally talented replacements.

RELATIONSHIP TO CUSTOMER ENGAGEMENT

One of the main problems with disengaged employees is that they are the primary source of inconsistent and unpredictable experiences for others, including customers and vendors. Maybe you have a good product, but that won't matter if a buyer calls customer service and the employee on the line is unhelpful and has a bad attitude. Or maybe the customer gets good service on the phone, but the staff at the bricks-and-mortar store is dismissive. These are negative experiences that move the dial toward disengagement and dissatisfaction. The toxicity of the disengaged can impact customers directly (through direct personal contact) and indirectly by triggering disengaged behaviors of other employees who in turn touch customers, leaving negative impressions.

Highly engaged employees create the great relationships that organizations want with customers. Because highly engaged employees behave in consistently positive ways, business owners can expect customer loyalty that's predictable and leads to improved business performance, return on investment, productivity, shareholder value, and profitability. It's a fairly simple equation, and it all starts with the leadership. If the most senior leaders are not committed (present at important meetings, walking the talk, validating success), if they don't buy in, the chances of an employee engagement initiative (training, new values, and norms) getting sustainable traction are virtually zero.

Engaged employees create more consistent and predictable positive experiences around the brand, which generate positive feelings in the customer's brain. "Feel good" neurotransmitters like dopamine and oxytocin are released when a person has consistently positive experiences; they feel good and they want more, so they return again and again. Customers become loyal and engaged most readily when their relationship with the brand, service, and employees is positive, consistent, and reliable. Who wouldn't want more of that?

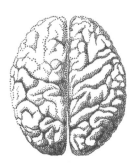

CHAPTER INSIGHTS

➴ Traditional management theory is based on routine job environments, but today's evolving workforce requires new, science-based models that draw out the best in people. The old way of managing from the top down just isn't as effective anymore.

→ With a growing economy and less talent available, leaders either need to pay people more to keep them, or—far more effectively—they need to create an environment where employees look forward to coming to work every day.

→ There are three common types of leaders today: A 1.0 Leader is traditional, hierarchal, and punitive. A 2.0 Leader is motivational and charismatic but relationally inconsistent. A 3.0 Leader is transformational, team-focused, and relational.

→ Employees are hardwired to have trustworthy social resources so that they do not have to work in isolation. In a healthy work environment, they can find these connections in multiple ways: with their peers, their manager, senior leaders of the organization, and the mission and vision of the company. When these strong attachments are in place, employees free up mental resources allowing for more productivity, innovation, creativity, and discretionary effort.

→ Disengaged employees have a disproportionately negative impact on an organization. Even if there is a higher percentage of engaged employees in a team, the disengaged tend to pull down the "A" players to the lowest common denominator.

CHAPTER ACTION STEPS

→ *Reflect:* Answer the question *"What does it feel like to work here?"* for yourself. What would your employees say? Your answer, and theirs, helps you define what your current culture is. Are you satisfied with that definition? Where do you see opportunities for improving the culture (increasing a felt sense of safety)?

→ *Act:* Lead by example for your team in holding disengaged employees accountable for their negative or disruptive behavior. By modeling core values and not allowing disengaged employees to hijack your team culture, you are setting the tone for your engaged employees to do the same.

→ *For Manager Resource Center subscribers:* Visit ManagerResourceCenter.com and review **Satisfaction vs. Engagement** in Step One of the Foundation section. Knowing the differences between the two will keep you on track as you develop new initiatives to deepen employee engagement.

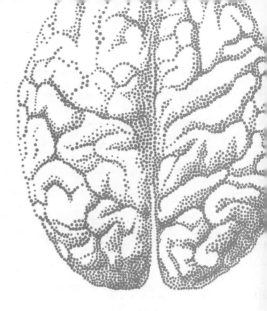

CHAPTER 6

POSITIVE LEADERSHIP

Every art and every investigation, and likewise every practical pursuit or undertaking, seems to aim at some good: hence it has been well said that the good is that at which all things aim.

—ARISTOTLE, *NICOMACHEAN ETHICS 1.1*

Positive Leadership, *noun.*
The strategic reliance on a positive bias to steer cultures toward conditions that support employee well-being, improve business outcomes like productivity and profitability, and align organizations with the science behind maximizing employee engagement.

"I only hear from my manager when she thinks I've made a mistake," a hotel worker told me in a team meeting with her peers, "and not once when I stay late, or help her out so she can leave early. You do good and you hear nothing. Make a mistake and it's all you hear. And now you ask me why I'm disengaged." Her coworkers in the meeting nodded their heads in agreement.

The fact is, human beings naturally perform better under positive circumstances, and nowhere is this more important than inside organizations. The research shows that positive leaders generate benefits to the individual employee, the team, and the organization. So why aren't more leaders relying on the proven benefits of positivity?

The traditional role of managers is to hold people accountable: to timelines, budgets, productivity, and a myriad of other factors. The mindset of management since at least the beginning of the Industrial Revolution has tended toward an enforcement model, an approach that implies that if employees are given any slack they will misbehave and underperform. This led to workplace conditions—existing even today in many organizations—that are hierarchical and punitive. It is essentially a fear-based approach where employees perform their duties under threat of some kind of punishment.

Employees endure this approach because they traditionally have gone to work out of financial necessity and fear of the stigma of being fired and the subsequent debilitating process of looking for a new job. As we discussed earlier in this book, those are precisely the conditions that existed in the United States and other industrialized countries for more than two hundred years. In environments where there are more people than jobs, it is possible to force people to work under punitive conditions and have them still show up. But those days are over, and managers need new, better, and science-based skills to lead and engage their employees going forward. Moving toward a positive leadership model will generate the most return in the least amount of time.

THE SCIENCE BEHIND POSITIVE LEADERSHIP

There is no longer any question that positive social interactions in the workplace are directly beneficial to employee wellness. But this has not always been the case. As recently as 2008, researchers at McGill University and the University of Michigan lamented in the *Academy of Management Review* that the approaches for analyzing workplace dynamics were too detached from the full human experience. "For organizational researchers, human physiology is a distant concern. We typically seek to understand social life in organizations using . . . [only] cognitive, affective, and behavioral explanations."[61]

They acknowledged that "most of our theories assume that workers are 'bodiless' or that the body is under the control of the mind. The result is that we don't know very much about how the body contributes to human action and capability." The authors argued for a "theoretical and practical view that more completely recognizes employees' embodied existence as a complicated and consequential bearer of the effects of organizational systems and the social interactions they cultivate."[62]

There is still a long way to go in the leadership ranks of today's organizations and in the field of organizational development on the road toward embracing a more holistic and realistic perspective on how the social ecosystems within teams, departments, and companies have direct consequences on the bottom line. The good news is leaders don't need a comprehensive understanding of these linkages; they can make considerable progress by simply making the environments they influence more positive.

---

61 Emily D. Heaphy and Jane E. Dutton, "Positive Social Interactions and the Human Body at Work: Linking Organizations and Physiology," *Academy of Management Review* 32, no. 1 (2008): 137–162.

62 Ibid, 138.

At the core of the nascent field of leadership science (as opposed to the well-established field of leadership practice) is an alignment with the neural hunger for safe and secure relationships. A key synonym for safety in this context is positivity, the quality or state of being positive. A positive relationship is far more likely to be seen as a reliable social resource than a negative one. In large part because the limbic system overemphasizes negativity (favoring threats that don't exist), leaders who interact with their direct reports through a positive frame free up metabolic capacity by reducing or eliminating those perceived threats so that more work gets done at a higher quality.

Negative leaders can get employees to do things. A fear-based model will work to a degree (we do respond to threats) but will never elicit an individual's best performance. Negative conditions such as a hierarchical, unavailable, passive-aggressive, or punitive manager can impel human behavior, but they create a level of relational and emotional toxicity that prevents employees from achieving their full potential. Negative motivational tactics are remarkably corrosive to the human spirit and will prevent organizations from achieving peak performance. These tactics are the primary drivers of workplace drama, poor performance, sabotage, and turnover (just to name a few).

NEGATIVE MOTIVATIONAL TACTICS ARE REMARKABLY CORROSIVE TO THE HUMAN SPIRIT AND WILL PREVENT ORGANIZATIONS FROM ACHIEVING PEAK PERFORMANCE.

In contrast, there is a growing body of research that demonstrates the measurable advantages of managers who are positive leaders, including improvements in individual behavior, team efficacy, and overall organizational performance. The phrase *positive leadership* captures a broad range of actions that leaders throughout the organization can take to create conditions that bring out the best in human behavior.[63] These conditions allow employees to thrive, not simply because the environment is positive but because the human brain is attracted to the positivity. In the absence of negativity, mental capacity improves, allowing the brain to thrive closer to its full capacity.

There are few management approaches that deliver as broad a range and level of increase in employee engagement as a singular focus on improving the positive conditions in organizations and teams. "Leadership has to do with relationships, the importance of which cannot be overstated. Leadership is an inherently relational, communal process."[64] Positive leaders will always be among the most important relational assets in any company seeking to achieve and maintain a high-performance culture. In addition to the individual benefits of positive leadership, the organization as a whole thrives under this approach. Research of sixteen different industries (including manufacturing, retail, financial services, health care, education, government, and not-for-profit, among others) conducted by Dr. Kim Cameron of the Stephen M. Ross School of Business at the University of Michigan found a significant relationship between "virtuousness" in the workplace—forgiveness, compassion, optimism, trustworthiness—and improvements in everything from profitability and productivity to quality and innovation, customer satisfaction and employee retention.[65] The results of firms

---

63 Jane Allyn Piliavin and Hong-Wen Charng, "Altruism: A Review of Recent Theory and Research," *Annual Review of Sociology* 16 (1990): 27–65.

64 Susan R. Komives, Nance Lucas, and Timothy R. McMahon, *Exploring Leadership* (San Francisco: Jossey-Bass, 2013).

65 Kim S. Cameron, "Organizational Virtuousness and Performance," in Kim S. Cameron, Jane E. Dutton, and Robert E. Quinn, eds., *Positive Organizational Scholarship* (San Francisco: Berrett-Koehler, 2003), pp. 48–65.

that showed the most improvement in scores pertaining to virtuousness also retained the highest levels of profitability, productivity, engagement, and employee and customer retention two years later.[66]

Positive emotions increase mental capacity, allowing employees to think more clearly and creatively and to act in more supportive, caring, and virtuous ways. How can we tap into these benefits as leaders? We ask managers in our Positive Leadership seminar what behaviors they consider the most effective. Here is the prioritized list of the top six:

1. The leader leads by example.

2. The leader is available and visible.

3. The leader mentors others.

4. The leader recognizes employee accomplishments.

5. The leader encourages others.

6. The leader listens well.

Positive leadership ties back to our earlier discussion of the limbic system and the fact that it favors false positives. As a result of the brain's hyper-vigilance to negativity and threat, it takes about five positive interactions to neutralize one negative. Numerous studies regarding workplace performance, when comparing positive statements (a proxy for trusted social resources) to negative statements, have found that this same ratio is found in high-performance teams. Negative statements include cynicism, criticism, disapproval, and sarcasm. Interactions representing positive statements include validation, encouragement, support, appreciation, and approval. This ratio of positive to negative statements was, by itself, more than

66 Kim S. Cameron and Jon McNaughtan, "Positive Organizational Change," *Journal of Applied Behavioral Science* 50: 445–462 (2014).

twice as powerful as any other factor in predicting organizational performance.[67]

The most effective way to improve the positive to negative ratio is not by increasing positive statements and interactions, oddly enough, but rather by reducing the negative. "I do get praise," an employee told me, "but it's hard to take in when most of what my supervisor tells me is how I'm failing." Instead of simply piling on more positives, the highest return on time and initiative invested in creating positive leadership is in identifying and removing organizational and interpersonal negatives.

ACCOUNTABILITY AS A POSITIVE LEADER: THE ABC METHOD

As a manager, most of the negatives in the workplace come while holding people accountable—but how does a manager hold people accountable without being negative? Learning this skill is essential in building and maintaining a high-performance culture. Providing feedback through a more positive frame is one of the most important shifts a leader (at any level) can make. There's a very simple three-step model we share with clients for holding people accountable in a way that won't trigger their defenses and doesn't sting.[68]

To help managers remember this approach, we refer to it as the *ABC method.*

---

67 Kim S. Cameron, Jane E. Dutton, and Robert E. Quinn, eds., *Positive Organizational Scholarship* (San Francisco: Berrett-Koehler, 2003).

68 For more on this approach, see *The Appreciative Inquiry Handbook: For Leaders of Change* by David L Cooperrider, Diana Whitney, and Jacqueline M. Stavros.

"A" stands for Appreciation.

Start the conversation with appreciation for something positive about the employee that relates to performance, behavior, or attitude.

"B" stands for Be Real.

Turn the discussion to what isn't going well to hold the employee accountable for their actions.

"C" stands for Curiosity.

Ask thoughtful questions. Inquire about ways their performance could have delivered a better outcome.

In the traditional scenario, a manager uses a punitive frame focusing on the individual's failure.

"You botched this up," "You've got to get this right or you're out of here," and "I'm really wondering if you're capable of doing this right" are just a few of the typical refrains in this top-down and negative frame. This kind of approach leads to a range of undesirable outcomes where the employee leaves the conversation feeling defeated, ashamed, angry, defensive, or resentful. Depending on the employee's personality, they may want to dig in and fight back or just crawl into a hole.

In contrast, let's hold someone accountable using the ABC method:

A (Appreciation): *"First of all, John, I want to thank you for the level of effort that you and your team put into this project. I know you all worked hard. I saw you and some of your team members here working late and on a few weekends, and I appreciate the level of effort that you all put into this."*

This appreciation needs to be unqualified. There can't be a "but"; there can't be a "however." This step is essential in preventing the employee from seeing the entire process as being unfair or unbalanced. Leaders tend to frame failures either as if failure were the intent of the individual from the outset or as if a single event represented overall failure. Employees, on the other hand, see the event in multiple parts—some of which may have been done quite well, with great integrity, and even with personal sacrifice. When a manager categorizes the entire process as a failure, they miss the opportunity to focus on the positive intent and admirable effort exercised. Finding this sliver of appreciation can be the hardest thing for the manager to come up with, especially if in the moment they're angry or full of their own anxiety around a failure or shortcoming. But the conversation must start by leveraging something positive.

B (Be Real): *"We didn't get where we wanted to with this project. We are well short of the outcome we set, and I'm disappointed about that. I suspect you and your team are also disappointed that we haven't achieved our end goal yet."*

The goal here is to let the person know in no uncertain terms that the project was not successful but to get the point across with less sting (shaming, blaming, demoralizing) than the previous, "old school" example. Also note the pronoun use—"*we* didn't get where we wanted to." The use of "we" acknowledges a sense of shared responsibility and the benefits of a relational frame around accountability (more on this in chapter 8).

Note that in the example the manager says, "I'm disappointed." The "I" pronoun is appropriate when managers can talk about their own emotional experience, such as "I am worried about how this reflects on the department . . ." Since we are hardwired as relational beings, the emotional state of respected peers and leaders can serve as a powerful pivot point for performance. By the end of the conversation, the person knows they are accountable, but they are far less likely to be angry and defensive.

C (Curiosity): *"John, I'm curious; if we're going to do this project again, and we probably will, what could we do differently to change the outcome? How could I have supported you and your team better, or what other factors might have been at play that caused us to not reach our goal? I don't expect you to have answers right now, but could we get together tomorrow over lunch and talk about what we could have done differently that would have allowed this project to be successful?"*

Ending with curiosity is the secret ingredient of this approach, primarily because it changes the trajectory of what the employee will do after the meeting. Instead of going home that night and updating their resume and complaining to their spouse about how unfairly they were treated, they are more likely to spend their time focusing on what could have been done differently, since they are answerable to that question tomorrow at lunch. But this isn't just a matter of changing the employee's frame of mind. It also entails a completely different approach to accountability and problem solving, one that involves the employee in an analysis of what they could have done differently to change the trajectory of the project's outcome. This process leads to personal and professional growth and can turn a point of failure into an opportunity for future success time and time again.

The conversation also needs to explore other possible factors that may have influenced the project outcome in addition to any one employee's performance. Where was the manager when things went sideways? What was the role of other staff or departments? Could the instructions for the task have been better? Would better training or equipment have changed the outcome? Including other potential factors (even if debunked) will help employees feel that the feedback was both thorough and fair.

The difference between what that employee does after the meeting in the first scenario and what they do after the meeting using the ABC method is vast. In the first, more punitive example, the employee leaves feeling defensive, dejected, or treated unfairly because it was such a one-sided approach. Depending on the severity, the employee might think they're about to get fired, that they need to leave the organization, and they're certainly not at their best or engaged in a remedy anywhere close to their full capacity.

There is another, long-term advantage of the ABC approach as the employee takes more ownership of their behavior, in this instance and in the future. They will now spend the next twenty-four hours trying to figure out what could have been done differently. The ABC method leaves the person feeling more optimistic, involved, and willing to look for solutions. The accountability conversation expands beyond correction into a teaching opportunity where the employee learns how to self-correct in the future.

When we explained the ABC method in one of our seminars, one CEO said, "You just explained what happened to me yesterday." One of his senior leaders made an enormous mistake that infuriated the CEO. "Everyone knows I'm a straight shooter, and I like to keep it real with all of my people, so I just ripped into Bob in front of his peers. I was furious."

Having just heard me talk about the ABC method, he knew he had made a big mistake. He then shared what happened when he got home the night of his tirade. "I was at my desk finishing up on some emails for the day when I heard a little bell tone on my computer, so I glanced over to see the pop-up message. It was an automated message from LinkedIn telling me Bob had just updated his profile."

In my meeting with the CEO, he was now visibly distraught, worried that Bob was going to quit. "I really screwed up, didn't I?" he said. "Well, he probably feels pretty bad right now," I replied. "You should give Bob a call right away and see what needs to be done to repair your relationship."

A key ingredient in the ABC approach is the leader's willingness to be vulnerable (not having all the answers; leading with concern and emotion) and be curious rather than assertive and punitive.

Now, what if the leader meets with the employee the following day at lunch and none of the recommendations the employee offers involve themselves? What if everything that could have been done differently should have been done by someone else? That's a problem! But here as well, an approach of vulnerability can deliver far more productive results than a simple accusation or admonition.

"John, I'm confused. Help me understand these ideas on your list. There are some valuable insights, but as I look over this list, I'm not seeing what *you* could have done differently. Help me understand your role as the project leader. What could *you* have changed?"

Starting with the frame of vulnerability, "Help me understand," diminishes defensiveness and encourages the employee to lean in and respond instead of getting defensive. The employee is not under attack—he or she is being queried.

The difference in framing is enormous in the felt experience of the person who is being held accountable. Managers with whom we work like this approach because it allows them to have accountability conversations with their direct reports without being overtly negative and critical. You actually can increase the number of valuable accountability conversations in your organization when you empower managers to have them without the negative spin and bite.

When moving to a more positive leadership style, including the ABC approach, you'll find there is a significant impact on your people:

- ✓ They work harder and perform better on the job.

- ✓ They display more mental acuity and make higher-quality decisions.

- ✓ They are more creative and flexible in their thinking.

- ✓ They are more adaptive and resilient after trials and trauma.

- ✓ They engage in more helping behaviors and citizenship activities.[69]

THE SURPRISING IMPACT OF POSITIVE LEADERSHIP

In addition to job performance, the research highlights that the leadership qualities of negative bosses—1.0 Leaders—over time exert a heavy toll on employees' health. And despite the way such leaders often rationalize and defend their stress-inducing, unsupportive style, the behaviors of a 1.0 Leader do not contribute to improved individual performance or organizational productivity.[70]

Chronic stress can result when someone must deal daily with a difficult boss, such as a 1.0 Leader. This kind of stress in the workplace has a direct impact on home life as well. When employees carry their stress from work into their personal lives, they magnify the toxicity by inadvertently introducing negativity at home. Such stress has been

69 Kim S. Cameron, *Positive Leadership: Strategies for Extraordinary Performance*, p. 71.

70 Rebecca Shannonhouse, "Is your boss making you sick?" *Washington Post*, retrieved on April 26, 2017, https://www.washingtonpost.com/national/health-science/is-your-boss-making-you-sick/2014/10/20/60cd5d44-2953-11e4-8593-da634b334390_story.html?utm_term=.590879388618.

linked to high blood pressure, sleep problems, and anxiety and is also associated with several unhealthy behaviors such as smoking, excessive use of alcohol, and overeating. Research has also linked the degree to which supervisors demonstrate fairness (such as giving timely feedback, including praise when warranted, and showing trust and respect) to employees' blood pressure. And a meta-study of 279 studies found a link between unfairness and mental health complaints such as depression.[71]

Here are some of the benefits of positive leadership for employees at home:

- living longer (by more than eleven years)
- succumbing to fewer illnesses
- a higher survival rate after a serious illness or accident
- staying married longer
- tolerating pain better[72]

Anything interpreted by the brain as threatening or negative consumes valuable and limited mental resources and produces a wide range of unhealthy physiological impacts. Negativity discourages productive, pro-organizational behaviors that would otherwise contribute to a high-performance culture and has a disproportional impact on individual and organizational competencies. Conversely, a positive (safe, predictable, relational) workplace culture delivers significant pro-engagement workplace outcomes. In the next two chapters we'll discuss how to implement actions supportive of positive leadership in a manager's daily interactions with colleagues and team members.

---

71 Ibid.

72 Cameron, *Positive Leadership: Strategies for Extraordinary Performance*, p. 71

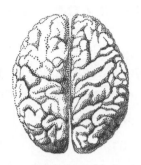

CHAPTER INSIGHTS

↪ Positive leadership encompasses a broad range of actions and behaviors that foster a thriving work environment. Positive leaders are relational, consistent, and supportive.

↪ In the brain, it takes five "positives" to neutralize one "negative," reflecting the disproportionate impact of negative events and experiences over positive ones. This five-to-one ratio is one of the most predictive characteristics of a high-performance team.

↪ Leaders can hold employees accountable without being negative by using the ABC method: Appreciate, Be Real, Show Curiosity.

↪ Stress that comes from working under a toxic manager or culture has implications beyond the office setting. Employees in these conditions are more likely to experience health concerns, marital problems, and substance abuse issues.

CHAPTER ACTION STEPS

➜ *Reflect:* Think about the way you typically communicate to those under your leadership. What do you think your positive-to-negative statement ratio is? What situations trigger your negative reactions? How can you approach those triggers with more self-awareness so that you can reduce the number of negative statements you make? How can you help others on the team shift to a more positive frame?

➜ *Act:* Often, negative statements and interactions come when something goes wrong. Many managers don't wait to get the full picture of the situation before rushing to judgment and negativity. Practice active listening and show curiosity by asking questions to uncover the situation fully before correcting an employee. When your employee feels heard and respected, the situation (and trusted relationship) can be maintained as you hold them accountable in a more positive way.

➜ *For Manager Resource Center subscribers:* Visit ManagerResourceCenter.com and download the **Weekly Planner for Positive Leaders** from your Toolkit. Use this checklist to more intentionally embed positive leadership practices into your daily routine.

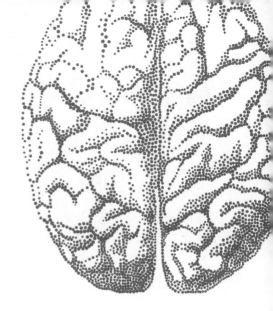

CHAPTER 7

VALIDATION, RECOGNITION, AND FEEDBACK

Every time you have to speak, you are auditioning for leadership.[73]
—JAMES C. HUMES

There are three main components an organization needs to have in place in order to effectively shift engagement: validation, recognition, and feedback.

Validation, recognition, and feedback are three of the most powerful tools available to managers and leaders to encourage a more positive work environment and effectively change the behaviors of employees and, more broadly, to improve the workplace culture. These touch points help us as humans, as herd animals, to know whether we're appreciated by the group, whether we're important to others, and whether others see and value our contributions. Great managers use these relational tools to improve and sustain high-qual-

---

73   James C. Humes, *The Sir Winston Method: The Five Secrets of Speaking the Language of Leadership* (New York: Morrow, 1991).

ity interpersonal relationships and strategically to improve performance and accountability.

I have found that managers are more likely to provide validation, recognition, and feedback when they understand the unique role of each of these touch points with employees. The goal of using these three motivational instruments is not gratuitous praise but rather a strategic understanding of employees' need to know that they are seen and valued, that their accomplishments are noticed and appreciated, and how they can improve.

VALIDATION

Validation, *noun | val•i•da•tion | \va-lə-dā-shən*
Validation is the unconditional acknowledgment of an individual's presence and intrinsic value as a human being. It is not dependent on task accomplishment; it is a process of predictable, consistent, and safe interactions that elevates the quality of relationships between individuals, the team, and other employees. It requires managers and leaders to slow down, lean in, and authentically care, listen, and respond from the heart. Tone of voice, facial expressions, direct eye contact, and being present in the moment all contribute to effective validation.

The process of valuing others is not contingent on specific achievements or lack thereof. People need to feel appreciated simply because they exist, because they are human beings. We all wake up every day in search of validation—the need to know "Am I noticed and valued?" We look for validation from our spouse, parents, friends, and colleagues, and when we get it we immediately feel more connected and innately safer. We do this intrinsically for each other as social animals, hardwired to recognize the presence (and significance) of the other. It is perhaps the most fundamental part of any relationship. Many managers, and certainly traditional management theories, ignore this form of communication—considering it so inconsequential that it doesn't even merit a mention, when in fact it should be a primary responsibility of every leader.

Nothing should be more second nature to a leader than acknowledging and recognizing the presence of others. Validation needs to be habitual, because its repetition increases its veracity—how it is believed by the recipient. It should also be given with a positive connotation (accompanied by a smile and eye contact, for example) to be most effective. These interactions do not require much from a manager other than consistency and predictability. In my seminars, managers identify conversational topics that can serve as great points of validation for their employees. Here are some primary themes that have emerged in our workshops: Managers can ask about weekend activities and family, offer a simple smile and "hello," practice active listening, discuss non-work-related topics, check in at the end of the day with a "have a good evening," and give high fives. These simple gestures allow managers to connect with their team members on a personal level and go a long way in creating a healthy culture of validation.

In order for this communication to come across as sincere, it's important to pay attention to how you're validating, not just what you're saying. Pay attention to these three components of your message:

word choice (specific and clear)

body language (smiling, good eye contact)

voice tone (warm tone, not rushed)

Effective validation should be:

- ✔ natural
- ✔ spontaneous
- ✔ sincere
- ✔ habitual

- ✔ relational
- ✔ unconditional
- ✔ informal
- ✔ frequent

Here are some helpful phrases to let others know they are valued:

- ✔ How were the soccer games this weekend?
- ✔ Tell me about your vacation!
- ✔ How can I help you today?
- ✔ What are you doing this weekend?
- ✔ Did you enjoy the concert you went to last night?

Creating a high-performance culture, where employees look forward to coming to work and are engaged when they get there, begins with the simple act of being noticed and valued.

RECOGNITION

Recognition, *noun | rec·og·ni·tion | \re-kig-ˈni-shən*
Recognition is conditional, based on three key elements: job performance, behavior, and attitude. It is a weekly conversation that begins with strengths (statements of praise and acknowledgment of a job well done) and can also include opportunities (needed improvements in performance, behavior, attitude). Whether done in person, electronically, or in writing, recognition is a positive expression of gratitude about a job well done, expectations exceeded, or the need to better align specific

behaviors with the achievement of personal, team, or corporate objectives.

High-performance cultures are built on a foundation of consistent, trusted, and frequent recognition. Recognition is largely the act of highlighting specific actions that both reinforce and support organizational goals and core values or spotlight contrary behaviors that need correction. Recognition can also be strategic, providing clear insight into which behaviors and values are held in high esteem by leadership. Great managers are typically very adept at providing meaningful recognition to their direct reports.

Sadly, one industry study pointed out that even though a significant majority of "best in class" organizations see employee recognition as extremely valuable in driving individual performance, only 14 percent of organizations provide managers with the necessary tools for rewards and recognition.[74] In another study, praise and commendation from managers was rated the top motivator for performance, beating out other non-cash and financial incentives, by a majority of workers (67 percent).[75] Clearly, recognition is a major driver of high-performance cultures, but we aren't doing enough to equip managers to do this well and often.

Effective recognition should be given frequently (ideally at least once a week to direct reports) and face-to-face (or by phone, in a thank-you note, or—as a last resort—in an email). It should be given quickly—the longer a manager waits to give recognition, the less it means to the recipient. It should also be specific—lots of details about why the praise was deserved. It can also be strategic and

---

74 Aberdeen Group, "The Power of Employee Recognition," November 2013, www.aberdeen.com.

75 Martin Dewhurst, Matthew Guthridge, and Elizabeth Mohr, "Motivating People: Getting Beyond Money," McKinsey Quarterly, November 2009.

include details around particularly desired behaviors (such as those congruent with core values).

Recognition should be given for a range of behaviors, for example, when an employee:

- ✔ exceeds expectations

- ✔ mentors others

- ✔ leans in to help when they see a need

- ✔ behaves in a way consistent with organizational core values

- ✔ innovates or offers suggestions on how to improve the effectiveness or efficiency of a process or product

- ✔ acts like an owner (such as conserving organizational resources, engaging fully in a project, showing initiative to improve the business, etc.)

- ✔ supports a positive workplace attitude and demeanor

The more traditional role of managers, to hold employees to high standards of job performance, is also important. But it can be accomplished more effectively by modifying the typically negative-toned, punitive, even shaming approach delivered by many managers. When giving corrective feedback, there are a few approaches that will improve outcomes:

Start with a strength. ("I really like how you have motivated the team so far, Sarah. Now let's see if we can pick up the pace a bit so we can finish on schedule.")

Redirect rather than admonish. ("I don't think you will be happy with the results of that approach, Maria. I would suggest . . .")

Come alongside the employee. ("Ken, I know this has been a tough project, and I would be frustrated if I were in your position. Let's work out a better approach together . . .")

Recognition can also be used to redirect an employee when they need to do something differently in order to achieve a better outcome. The objective is not to pamper the employee; it is instead to recognize that some portion of their effort was well intended (and executed), just not all. When leaders only focus on failure, employees are more likely to describe the process as unfair and to become defensive or despondent. The 3.0 Leader is more interested in redirecting future behavior than blaming a direct report for past behavior. If this recognition opportunity becomes too detailed, it probably means that a more formal feedback conversation should be scheduled (see the next section on feedback).

Here are some phrases to use when recognizing employees in a variety of situations, regarding continuous improvement, values, exemplary performance, and building stronger relationships:

Continuous Improvement

- ✓ I am always looking for ways we can improve what we do—and you've just given me a great new opportunity.

- ✓ We are trying to continuously improve. Thanks for helping the team find such an innovative approach to the old process.

Values

- ✓ You seem to have such passion for what you do—I just want you to know your attitude is appreciated.

- ✓ Respect is one of our core values. Thank you for demonstrating so much of that value in your work on this assignment.

- ✓ That's a very innovative solution to the problem. It's nice to see one of our core values implemented so effectively.

- ✓ When you are here, you add a positive vibe that I can tell encourages other members of the team to do the same.

Exemplary Performance

- ✓ You're a very quick study; I really appreciate how fast you learned the requirements of this job.

- ✓ We're so glad you've joined the team. Please let me know if there is anything I can do to help you in the onboarding process.

- ✓ Great to have you here. Please come to me if you have any questions. My door is always open.

- ✓ Every time I review your work I become more impressed with you.

- ✓ You just made a tough situation much easier to handle. Thank you!

Building Stronger Relationships

- ✓ I appreciate how you handled that situation. You are very calm, and I think that helped us get a quick resolution of the issue.

- ✓ You really know how to read social cues, and that helps us as a team be more collaborative with other departments. Thank you for helping us build strong bridges.

- ✓ I admire the way you connect with other people. You make them feel comfortable and at ease so quickly.

- A lot of our success depends on the quality of the relationships we have, both internally and externally with our vendors and customers. You are a role model for how to handle it well.

- You really seem to care about the other people on the team. It shows, and it really helps the team dynamic.

When I ask managers in our workshops what employee behaviors they could recognize more often, these top themes emerge: volunteering to help out others on the team, coming in early or working outside of normal business hours, working collaboratively to achieve end goals, going above and beyond what is expected, and demonstrating behavior reflecting company core values.

Leaders at all levels in the organization can increase employee engagement by looking for and speaking up when they see examples of employee discretionary effort and performance that is well aligned with company goals and core values. The behaviors they look to recognize don't need to be extraordinary (there won't be enough of them), just exemplary (admirable and commendable).

FEEDBACK

Feedback, noun | feed·back | \ˈfēd-bak\
Feedback is a confidential one-on-one meeting that should take place once a month. It is a conversation about job performance, behavior, and attitude—whether it exceeds, meets, or falls short of expectations. Feedback serves as a critical insight for employees on how their performance is viewed, as well as an opportunity to coach and inspire new behaviors that will improve outcomes.

Feedback, ideally, is an ongoing process, not an event. Since the human brain is hardwired to assess how we are valued by the people who matter most to us at home and work—including our supervisor—we want to know where we stand just about every minute of the day. Managers who give regular feedback to their direct reports will have more highly engaged teams as long as that feedback is authentic, constructively focused, and supportive.

Managers need to understand that feedback is more than a one-on-one meeting scheduled periodically (typically infrequently). When done well, feedback is a consistent and predictable exchange of expectations, validation, and recognition between the leader and their direct reports.

The best feedback is constructive; it feels supportive to the recipient, not punitive or demeaning. Holding employees accountable for what they do is essential, but great managers will find ways to do so in a way that is both corrective and supportive. Like validation and recognition, feedback should also be consistent and predictable. Leaders at all levels need to be more consistent and predictable in all of their behaviors, especially when it relates to the tone and frequency of feedback provided to staff.

Many managers assume that feedback only applies to situations representing a problem or a shortfall in performance or behavior. In addition to addressing areas of concern, it should also be given to acknowledge high-quality performance, celebrate success, and acknowledge personal initiative and discretionary effort. If done well, feedback is an essential element in answering the innate need to know if we are valued and how we can increase our value, and to share our hopes, needs, and concerns about our role in the organization.

In spite of its importance in better guiding and aligning employee performance, most organizations (and managers) conduct the process ineffectively and far too infrequently (only once or twice a year). The infrequency of these vital conversations goes against the neuroscience research that clearly demonstrates that the brain is looking for regular feedback that answers the hardwired (and constant) question "Am I seen and valued for my contributions?"

Two factors typically drive the traditional performance review process: (1) a mandate from the human resources department, and (2) the notion that by merely receiving "feedback," employee performance will improve. The first driver is now changing in many organizations, where the annual performance review is either significantly retooled or dropped altogether.[76] The assumptions behind the second driver have been historically untrue due to the clumsy and transactional (check-the-box) way the meeting is conducted.

In fact, we searched for the scientific foundation or theory that supports the efficacy of annual performance reviews and could not find any. The process emerged in the early 1900s and perhaps was marginally sufficient in an era of assembly lines and rote tasks. In both execution and frequency, it is largely ineffective and insufficient for today's more sophisticated jobs and employees.

The traditional feedback process can actually do more harm than good. A deeper understanding of the performance review process led researchers in the 1990s to conclude that the procedure "can impair performance and that the processes through which feedback interventions affect performance require more than simple explanations."[77] These researchers discovered that at least one in three performance reviews delivered negative outcomes.

76 Peter Cappelli and Anna Tavis, "The Performance Management Revolution," *Harvard Business Review,* October 2016.

77 Avraham N. Kluger and Angelo DeNisi, "Feedback Interventions: Toward the Understanding of a Double-Edged Sword," *Current Directions in Psychological Science* 7, no. 3 (1998).

Lacking a firm science-based need underlying the role of performance appraisals, I believe the fields of human behavioral science and neuroscience are the most reliable resources for critically important insights on how to maximize the effectiveness of formal and informal feedback. Gathering and presenting these insights, in fact, is a key goal of this book.

LINKING CORE VALUES TO THE FEEDBACK PROCESS

It's vital to connect your organization's core values to the recognition and feedback process. Doing so makes core values more relevant, links often abstract words to specific behaviors, and increases the chance of sustained behavioral change. For example, an employee will be more receptive to changing what they do because they see it as having integrity (a value), rather than because their manager told them to do it.

Here are some sample core values and the key behaviors to help you identify when an employee is practicing those core values:

Respect: Responds professionally to leadership requests and needs; treats everyone fairly, professionally, and with dignity; uses appropriate body language such as direct eye contact; makes appropriate grooming and clothing choices.

Collaboration: Works well in a team; completes tasks in a professional and timely manner; leans in to help others before being asked.

Positive: In demeanor, the employee smiles, greets others, and uses positive energy. In language, the employee frames conversations with supportive words. In creating a safe environment, the employee interacts with people in a consistent and predictable way.

Quality: Understands the steps and procedures for the job functions they perform; focuses on doing tasks to the best of their ability and in congruence with the goals and values of the team and organization.

Service: Thinks of the team more than themselves; goes above and beyond the job description or typical expectations in order to do the job right the first time; helps others in times of need.

Customer focus: Understands the relationship between product or service quality and the customer's experience; sees his or her daily objective as more than going through the motions to earn a paycheck and instead thinks about exceeding customer expectations; performs as if the customer were right next to him or her.

Trust: Behaves consistently and predictably; follows through and completes tasks with integrity; values fellow employees for more than the work they produce.

MONTHLY FEEDBACK

As a standalone, yearly procedure, the annual review is dead. Instead, performance reviews should be conducted at very regular intervals. Somewhere between the customary annual appraisal and the brain's constant need to know how it is valued, leaders need to find the time to provide the confidential conversation about performance, behavior, and attitude. Some organizations do it every quarter, some bimonthly. My preferred interval is once a month (depending on the number of direct reports).

When leaders at any level sit down for an intentional, one-on-one conversation with each of their direct reports on a monthly basis, they are not only able to keep performance concerns at bay (by addressing them right away and regularly), but they are also able to help their team members plan, prioritize, and achieve small and big milestones more easily over time.

Think of the different topics for your monthly feedback meeting in terms of altitude. Feedback about daily behavior and performance should be at a low altitude (a "fifty-foot view"). This part of the conversation is directly tied to the employee's specific actions, attitude, and presence. At a medium altitude (the "fifteen-thousand-foot view"), the conversation turns to the employee's progress on and contributions to project goals, quality of team interactions, and their ability to collaborate and delegate, for example. The highest altitude (the "thirty-thousand-foot view") is about the big picture—the employee's larger priorities, goals, and challenges in their current job, as well as in their personal and professional aspirations, and how they want to grow and be challenged in the organization. This is a perfect time to talk to each employee about how they are doing in the organization—and how you can support their growth and development inside your company as well.

Here's an example of what a monthly feedback conversation might look like.

The fifty-foot view: Daily behavior and performance

Before the meeting, reflect on:

❷ How does this employee show up to work every day? On time? Positive attitude?

❷ How does she interact with her teammates? Is she collaborative and helpful to others?

❷ What core values of our organization does she regularly demonstrate?

❷ Is she connected to the organization's mission and vision?

During the meeting, discuss your reflections
and consider asking questions like:

❷ How do you feel this past month has gone in your role on the team?

❷ Are there any other issues that we ought to be aware of or thinking about for you?

❷ Is there anything I can do to support you more?

The fifteen-thousand-foot view:
Project progress and goals

Before the meeting, reflect on:

❷ Looking back, what progress have I been able to identify since last month's feedback meeting?

❷ In what areas has he contributed well to our team?

❷ Looking forward, what priorities do I see as critical for him to tackle this month?

During the meeting, discuss your reflections
and consider asking questions like:

❓ Is there anything I can do to support you as you pursue your goals this month?

❓ Can you walk me through your decision-making process in this situation?

❓ What is your time frame for achieving these goals?

❓ What's the driving force behind this initiative?

❓ Did we accomplish what we hoped this past month?

❓ How do you feel this project/initiative/situation will further our mission and goals?

❓ What other team members or departments will you need to collaborate with this month to help you achieve these goals?

The thirty-thousand-foot view: Big-picture priorities and challenges, for their job and their own growth

Before the meeting, reflect on:

❓ What do I see as some of the biggest areas of growth for this employee?

❓ What opportunities can I tap into to help her grow? (For instance, "I think she is ready for a leadership role, but it isn't time for a promotion yet. I could put her as team lead for the new initiative on . . .")

❷ How did they answer these questions last month? What do I need to follow up on in this conversation based on the previous conversation?

❷ As the leader, what kind of feedback would be helpful for me from this employee?

During the meeting, discuss your reflections
and consider asking questions like:

❷ What do you see as your most significant opportunities for growth over the next several months/year? How do you want to be challenged?

❷ What are your biggest priorities this quarter?

❷ As you think about the future of your role and our organization, what are you excited about?

❷ What is a way you'd like to grow personally or professionally here? How can I help you be successful with that?

❷ What are major challenges you see yourself facing in the coming months?

❷ What might you need to let go of in order to move forward and accomplish your goals? How can I help you with that?

❷ How can I do a better job supporting you, leading this team, and helping you meet your objectives?

❷ What would be a helpful follow-up to this meeting?

FEEDBACK FOR A TRIGGERING EVENT

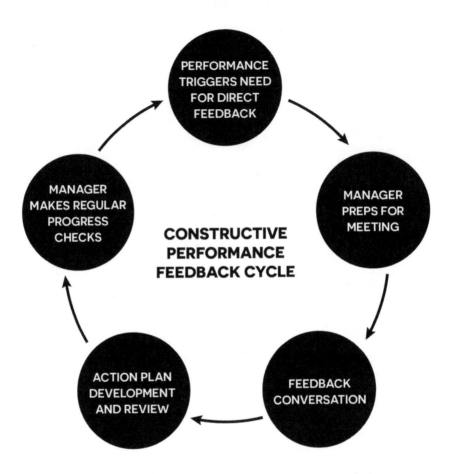

When managers see feedback as a process instead of an event, it feels more consistent and predictable to employees. This feedback cycle is specifically designed to respond to singular examples of an employee's behavior or performance that trigger the need for a feedback conversation.

The Feedback Cycle diagram highlights the fact that effective feedback is a process, not an event or an annual meeting. While performance reviews should be conducted at regular intervals, there may be cases that I refer to as a triggering event, where a feedback conversation needs to occur immediately. In this situation, the feedback must be timely. It should follow the event or trigger within a few days of the event's occurrence—the sooner the better. The meeting should be held privately and confidentially—never admonish someone publicly. Even if others (and the facts) support your anger, there will be long-lasting negative impressions about your leadership style if you make a scene when providing feedback.

This conversation should occur after you've had a chance to collect the relevant facts or details from multiple sources. Getting agreement on the details is an important step (but rarely sufficient for a solution). You should also give yourself a chance to calm your own anxiety (or anger) related to the event. Nothing will trigger a person's defensiveness more quickly and deeply than walking into a highly charged, overtly negative environment.

WHEN NOT TO GIVE FEEDBACK

- ❌ You are upset or angry.
- ❌ You don't have all the facts. There are at least two sides to every story.
- ❌ You want to punish.
- ❌ When others are around.
- ❌ When the triggering event is not timely.
- ❌ You haven't sought the employee's approval for a meeting.

Once you're able to ask in a calm—even supportive—tone, seek the employee's permission to talk about the event. For example, "Rebecca, this feels important. Can we talk about it?" This last point is important. It isn't because you need their permission; it is because the question allows them to exercise a choice regarding the conversation. It changes the frame from something that is done *to* them to a meeting that is done *with* them. The employee, in effect, has said, "Sure, we can talk about this."

In preparing for the feedback conversation, the leader should consider some of the following:

- ❓ Why do I feel compelled to have a feedback conversation with the employee?

- ❓ I have done my homework: gathered as many details about the event or issue as possible, asked questions, and listened with an open mind.

- ❓ I have identified the behavior(s) I want to talk about and how they relate to the organization's core values.

- ❓ I am not rushing to judgment. I am trying to understand not only what happened but why it happened so that I can get to the root issue.

- ❓ What are the employee's professional and personal goals in the organization?

- ❓ Have I identified what I need to do differently going forward to better support the employee and team success?

Once fully prepared, have the feedback conversation with the employee. Be sure to think systemically about the event, seeing what happened as a part of a continuum, a process. If an employee failed at a task, there are often broader contributing issues (insufficient training, poor supervision, inadequate milestones to catch problems, etc.). Be sure to use the pronoun "we" rather than "you," as in: "We need to figure out how this can be done more effectively next time."

Also, be sure you have the right framing: You're giving "constructive feedback," not "constructive criticism." Remember, anything overtly negative is a potential threat to the brain, and cognition (and IQ) drops.

The meeting should be followed by mutual agreement on an action plan that includes the next steps and a timeline. Reaching mutual agreement ensures aligned expectations, and the action plan gives the employee a structured game plan for how to move forward with clear milestones.

A critical final step is for the manager to make regular progress checks (which should also include validation and recognition) over time.

The steps to providing feedback are as follows:

I. Employee's performance triggers a need for direct feedback:

- Employee either exceeds or falls short of expectations/requirements.

- Manager observes or learns of triggering behavior.

- Other employees ask for an intervention/recognition.

II. Prep for meeting:

- Collect facts and relevant context.

- Ask for permission to meet.

- Select a safe venue ensuring confidentiality.

- List specifics for praise or needed changes.

III. Hold the feedback conversation:

- Be curious, listen, take notes.

      □ Begin with strengths, maintain as positive a frame as possible.

      □ Find mutual agreement on details, context.

      □ Get mutual agreement on next steps, timing.

IV. Develop and review the action plan:

      □ Come to a mutual agreement on goals, next steps.

      □ Create a timeline.

      □ Coach and support.

V. Make regular progress checks with your employee:

      □ Coach.

      □ Validate.

      □ Encourage.

      □ Insist on accountability for milestones, goals.

EFFECTIVE FEEDBACK SHOULD INCLUDE THE FOLLOWING:

- ✔ specificity
- ✔ opportunity for growth and advancement
- ✔ mutual understanding of the details and agreement on next steps
- ✔ achievable goals
- ✔ a felt sense of safety
- ✔ respect for all parties
- ✔ a connection to core values

- a conversation with active listening

- an action plan with timeline and follow-up

- a time frame for commitments to be met and reviewed

- an understanding that facts rarely portray the complete story

- a high value placed on relationships and influencing human behavior

- both parties coming to the meeting prepared to take notes

FEEDBACK FOR ACTIVELY ENGAGED PERFORMERS

Top performers pride themselves on their quality of work and typically go above and beyond whenever they can. As a result, they often are particularly sensitive about receiving feedback, especially if it is perceived as negative or critical. On the other hand, these "A" players are usually open—even anxious—to receive input on how they can do things even better. How managers frame this communication sets the tone for productive feedback.

Here are guidelines for providing feedback to top performers in your organization:

Frequency. The more engaged the employee, the more frequently they should receive feedback and recognition for what they do. Ironically, because these "A" players are perceived as being so self-sufficient and internally motivated, managers often neglect them, mistakenly thinking that they have little need for information about how their performance is viewed.

Gratitude. One of the primary nutriments for "A" players is to be recognized and validated by their manager or supervisor. Top-level performance is rarely triggered exclusively by extrinsic motivators like salary and benefits (although those can be positive contributing factors). Powerful intrinsic motivators typically drive high performers, and recognition based on this intrinsic motivation is a compelling reward.

Continuous improvement. Top performers want to improve their skills regularly to stay relevant and to grow their value to the organization. They are firm believers in the concept of continuous improvement and/or self-improvement, so managers should use this feedback element strategically.

Goal identification. All employees benefit from a clear understanding of goals expected of them by the organization and leadership. Actively engaged performers often resonate with goals that involve solving tough problems or that feel like an exciting opportunity. When identifying stretch goals with top performers, make sure you believe they can be achieved—because the benefit is less with the stretch than with the "we did it!" celebration upon completion.

Value to the organization. Top performers typically have a healthy perspective around their value to the organization. It never hurts to make that an explicit part of the conversation with these "A" players. Validate their value first, then explore ways to lift it to the next level.

FEEDBACK FOR ACTIVELY DISENGAGED PERFORMERS

Inevitably, leaders will find themselves in a feedback session with low performers—employees who either just don't care or seem unable to deliver a consistently positive and productive performance when at work. Maintaining a positive frame in these often challenging discussions can be difficult and can even feel counterintuitive in the face of a high level of corrective need.

Here are guidelines for providing feedback to the most disengaged performers in your organization:

Safety. Establish an environment of safety at the beginning of the conversation. Since the brain is hyper-sensitive to situations that feel threatening and negative, our hardwired defense mechanisms can be easily triggered. Once someone becomes defensive, it is difficult to create positive, constructive outcomes.

Here are a few suggestions and phrases for creating a felt sense of safety in formal feedback settings:

Ask for permission. "Is it okay if you and I have a conversation around a performance issue that I am concerned about?"

Reaffirm the individual's importance. "I hope you know how important your contributions are to the team. We all rely on you to help us be successful. I don't want you to underestimate that."

Frame the conversation. "If I were in your position, I know I would want to know any time something I've done can be improved upon. I never like being in the dark about my performance. It's hard to get better when the people around you aren't providing some constructive feedback."

Transparency helps. Remember that most employees suffer from a lack of information regarding their performance, so the opportunity for an honest, supportive, and constructive conversation around their performance will be seen as helpful rather than hurtful. An employee might respond, "I had no idea it was so important to you how I left my workstation at the end of the shift. Thanks for letting me know. I can take care of that right away."

Stay cool. If you are angry or upset about the situation you are discussing, take some time (preferably overnight) to de-escalate. The more emotionally charged you are, the less likely your conversation will have a productive outcome.

Self-reflection. Provide an opportunity for your team to self-reflect. You need to understand those areas of employee performance where they feel they have given their best. It is often surprising to discover where an employee feels they have made their most important contributions. Be sure to validate and recognize those areas of accomplishment, especially if they were not included in your gratitude. Ask the employee to list what they consider their strengths to be. Once they have identified a few items, ask them if they are dedicating their full capacity to those strengths—or do they have more to give under the right conditions?

Continuous improvement. Introduce this framework into the conversation to help position the feedback as a conversation about new areas for growth and development, rather than criticism. Even less-engaged staff can become more energized within the concept of continuous improvement and/or self-improvement.

Mutual agreement. If there is a specific performance issue being discussed, consider beginning with an agreement on the facts and details of the issue. There is always another side to every story, so simply be present with the person and listen to their perspective and acknowledge that you understand it. Then share your view of the same situation and come to some mutual agreement on what actually happened.

Impact and consequences. Once there is agreement on the situation, identify from your perspective some of the consequences. What was the impact on:

❷ the customer experience?

❷ other members of the team or another group/team in the organization?

❷ you as the leader of the group?

❷ product quality?

❷ the brand, the company's reputation?

Be sure to include values-oriented and emotional consequences related to the performance issue. Underperformers will often argue about the facts or the details, but they cannot argue with your felt experience or that of others on the team. "Tom, I felt disappointed and let down by your performance." Because the conversation is about your feelings, the employee can't respond with "No you didn't, you weren't disappointed." People will usually also respond more effectively to the values-oriented or emotional impacts than they will to facts and details. "Mary, integrity is very important to both of us and everything we do as a team and company, so I want to explore how we can improve on that issue." "Sam, the whole team was disappointed; they felt let down by what you did, and I think we have some repair opportunities that we can work on together to help us move forward."

Compensation. The actively disengaged almost always blame their underperformance on issues related to compensation. The more disengaged the employee, the more often they use compensation as their excuse. Ask them if they can set aside the compensation issue for a moment and just focus the conversation on the level and tone of energy they bring to work every day. You could point out that other employees, paid the same, show up at work with a different demeanor and dedication to their daily tasks. "When you think about your own performance when you come to work every day, money aside for just a moment, what do you see as the roadblocks preventing you from being more engaged?" You might also point out that changes in rewards and compensation usually *follow* consistently impressive performance.

Value to the organization. Identify the ways the employee can increase their value to the team and the organization. This is an important frame for the conversation. "I would like us to work together to identify ways you can become even more valuable to the organization. I want to help maximize your value to the team and the company."

Goal identification. Allow your direct reports to identify future goals that are important to them. Rather than telling employees what you think their future goals should be, identify what they see as key objectives or where they feel their most important growth areas reside. Make sure you incorporate, to some degree, their aspirational goals around their professional development and value to the company, in addition to your own goals for them.

THE FEEDBACK ACTION PLAN

The goal of an action plan is to create clarity and transparency regarding what is expected of the employee and how they will be evaluated on meeting those expectations. It is also forward looking, and somewhat aspirational, rather than restrictive and punitive in nature.

One place to begin the development of a customized action plan for a specific employee is to look at the components of your organization's formal performance review. Think of the full annual performance review as a master list from which you can select specific elements that are the most relevant for that employee over the next six months. It is critically important that the action plan be focused on three or four key items in the near term so that the employee can maintain a clear focus. Including too many items on an action plan diffuses energy and makes each item less likely to be achieved.

One important aspect of the action plan is to show regular progress for the employee and eventually to claim success and take those items off the list so that new points of focus can be added.

An action plan is not a check-the-box exercise. Action plans need to be active, vibrant documents that identify goals and objectives and recognize them once achieved. Subsequent meetings also need to be scheduled to mutually assess and agree on progress achieved.

I've given a lot of attention to this chapter because our data from measuring employee engagement in organizations reveals a consistent message—employees are starving for validation, recognition, and feedback. The questions in our assessment tool regarding these issues consistently deliver the lowest results. We believe employee engagement can increase significantly if leaders throughout the organization simply focus on daily validation, weekly recognition, and a monthly constructive feedback conversation.

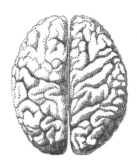

CHAPTER INSIGHTS

↪ Validation is the unconditional acknowledgment of another person's presence and value. Leaders need to communicate simple statements of validation every day with their employees.

↪ Recognition is conditional; it is the acknowledgment of an employee's performance, behavior, or attitude. Employees need to receive specific and timely recognition from their manager at least once a week.

↪ Effective feedback is a confidential, one-on-one conversation that takes place monthly between a manager and employee. These monthly conversations create clarity, focus, and a regular opportunity for two-way communication.

CHAPTER ACTION STEPS

→ *Reflect:* Of the three critical types of communication (validation, recognition, feedback) which do I need to be more intentional with? Do I validate my employees daily? How often do I offer intentional recognition? Am I giving enough feedback to each of my employees?

→ *Act:* Building a habit of regular validation, recognition, and feedback takes intentionality. Add a meeting notice or reminder to your calendar to check in with and recognize each of your employees. Handwrite one or two of your employees a thank-you note for going above and beyond this week. Set up your next one-on-one with each one of your direct reports. Follow the outline of a monthly feedback conversation found in this chapter.

→ *For Manager Resource Center subscribers:* Visit ManagerResourceCenter.com and download the **Feedback Action Plan** from your toolkit to foster collaboration between you and your employees when setting goals and objectives.

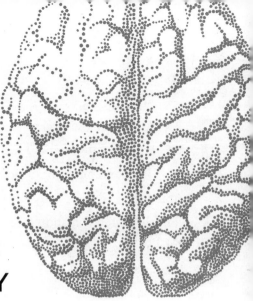

CHAPTER 8

ACCOUNTABILITY

A body of men holding themselves accountable to
nobody ought not to be trusted by anybody.

— THOMAS PAINE

The word *accountability* first appears in Norman, England, during the thirteenth century, but its roots go back much further. Scholars trace the etymology to ancient Egypt, where account giving was related to money lending, and governance was tied to the notion of holding people *to account*. The key point for leaders is that accountability is always achieved in relationship to something else. That is, employees are accountable for a reason; there must be a motivation within them strong enough to compel their behavior and performance in the direction leaders want.

The motivation to go to work traditionally pivoted around job security; in today's workplace, leaders need to work with other "pivot" points—like relationships (you care about the team and they are counting on you), values (I know you are a person of great integrity), and aspirations (I know you want that promotion), for example. Organizations are social ecosystems, and if leaders want to engender a workplace culture built on a foundation of accountability, they need to see accountability as more than simply responsibility to task accomplishment.

The contemporary business context for accountability, "responsible for what you do and able to give a satisfactory reason for it," is far too limited.[78] It should be defined more accurately from a behavioral perspective as something like this: *having a standard or value compelling enough to influence personal performance in ways beneficial to the organization and congruent with established goals and objectives.*

The associated word, *responsibility*, on the other hand, is more narrowly defined as "a duty to take care of something."[79] This definition is also too limited, because trying to motivate behaviors in beneficial ways based on a sense of duty alone (a required task or a legal or moral obligation) may have been sufficient in Workplace 1.0 to compel individual and collective performance, but it will not be enough in Workplace 3.0. More and more, leaders will want to appeal to more deeply held motivations connected to meaning, purpose, and fulfillment.

THE IMPORTANCE OF ACCOUNTABILITY

Being held accountable is a critical need in human systems where work needs to get done efficiently, with high quality, on time, and within budget. This isn't simply an operational concern—it also has a major impact on employee engagement and the overall culture.

Accountability makes a workplace social ecosystem safer to work in and increases the chances of employees being successful. When

---

78 *Cambridge Business English Dictionary* (Cambridge: Cambridge University Press, 2011).

79 Ibid.

employees arrive at work engaged and accountable, outcomes and behaviors are more predictable, expectations are more likely to be realized (and exceeded), and plans, schedules, and budgets become more reliable. Accountability is a magnet and amplifier for good behavior, positive outcomes, and top performers.

ACCOUNTABILITY IS A MAGNET AND AMPLIFIER FOR GOOD BEHAVIOR, POSITIVE OUTCOMES, AND TOP PERFORMERS.

Alternatively, imagine an environment where people are constantly pushing back deadlines, making excuses, or not showing up with their whole self for work (you may not have to imagine too hard)—and where disengaged behavior isn't addressed or dealt with. It's extremely frustrating for employees who give their best, on time and every time, to work in this kind of environment. When accountability is compromised, high standards collapse and "A" players become frustrated and are significantly more likely to underperform and, if the condition persists, to quit. Employees across the board lose their incentive to perform at full capacity, and subpar performance becomes the norm, protected by excuses, finger pointing, and blame.

Accountability, like employee engagement, pivots around managers. Earlier I mentioned that Gallup's research determined that about 70 percent of the fluctuation in workplace engagement is directly attributed to managers. Our experience tells us the same is true for accountability. Managers and senior leaders are responsible for establishing the conditions (relationships, values, aspirations) that encourage employees to be accountable.

OBSTACLES TO ACCOUNTABILITY

Organizations can enforce some level of accountability via punishment (risk of job loss, shaming in front of peers). Although it should be obvious by now I am not endorsing that approach, it is, nevertheless, possible to threaten people into accomplishing tasks in a specific way. You might remember the quotation from Alain de Botton's book *The Pleasures and Sorrows of Work* that opens chapter 1: "For most of human history, the only instrument needed to induce employees to complete their duties energetically and adroitly was the whip." This symbol of foreboding, the whip, has been used since at least ancient Rome. But while fear and intimidation may compel your employees to stay on task, it is far less likely they will do so in a positively discretionary way. Ideally, as leaders and managers, we would like employees to be accountable to:

- ✔ the values they hold dear
- ✔ themselves and their family
- ✔ their tasks and responsibilities
- ✔ the team
- ✔ their leader
- ✔ the organization
- ✔ the organization's mission and vision
- ✔ the organization's customers and other stakeholders

Sometimes, you'll encounter an employee or a team that tends to avoid direct responsibility for their behavior or outcomes. The following obstacles can easily impede the accountability you want to see in your team.

Individual Employee Obstacles

There is no such thing as irrational behavior. You may read that and think, "Yeah, right! You clearly haven't met my [insert "irrational" personal connection here]." But it's true! The full story on all the neural mechanisms driving behavior remains a mystery, but we do know this—there is a reason, a motivation behind every action we take. Nothing is done randomly; the apparent irrational action you saw someone do made perfect sense to his neural networks at the time. It may not have been a conscious mental conversation, but when the brain initiates action, it has a purpose. For example, we don't think, "I'm angry, so I think I will yell and be short with my team members for the next ten minutes to get out my frustration," yet there is a definite mental intention that triggered the outburst. This understanding will provide important context for the next section.

There are categories of behaviors that typify a lack of account-ability, such as learned helplessness, a victim mentality, and grudge collecting, that we have seen in just about every client company. CEOs and managers in our workshops regularly comment on and complain about the debilitating impact of these behaviors on the individual, the team, and the organization. The traditional way of dealing with these attitudes is endurance (create workarounds), pun-ishment (shape up or ship out), and shaming (go put on your big-boy pants), among others. In addition to the ABC approach I outlined in chapter 6, I would like to offer a different approach for some of the most common categories of unaccountable behavior.

Learned Helplessness

When employees don't feel they have control over a situation or they underestimate their own ability to influence a situation, they are often demonstrating learned helplessness. When people have experienced failure or poor performance repeatedly, some will eventually believe there is nothing they can do to improve the situation. "I could stay late and finish this, but it won't be right; it never is," for example, or "My opinion won't make any difference—everyone else is so much smarter than me."

What You Need to Do

When an employee has convinced herself that she has little or no control over a situation, your goal is to shift the attitude. The employee typically underestimates her own ability to influence a more positive outcome. Here are a few approaches you might consider.

Listen carefully. Active listening is a critical component in building a person's communication, confidence, and self-esteem. There are three parts to active listening: being present (fully in the moment—no distractions), understanding (seek clarity, nod in affirmation), and being responsive (validate, empathize).

> **Example:** You might say, "I really appreciate you bringing this to my attention. I know it can be hard to speak up when things aren't going smoothly. It sounds like you would like to implement a new strategy to minimize errors on this project. How can I help?"

Be curious. There is more to being curious than asking questions. The definition includes another component—eagerness. To be truly curious is to be eager to learn or know something. In this context, the tone and personal demeanor of the manager asking the questions is vital. Questions need to be asked with positive intent, with an authentic desire to come alongside the employee to better understand what they mean (not just what they say). Another benefit of being curious is the underlying message it sends to the recipient—that you care enough about them and their experience to slow down, be present, and converse with them. It is a useful example of validation, and the conversation often becomes rich with opportunities for recognition as well.

Reframe. Work with the employee to consider another perspective by explaining the situation in a more positive way; for example, as a short-term event rather than a permanent state, as limited to one specific circumstance rather than widespread, or as something that could have happened to anyone and not just to them.

> **Example:** If your employee says, "Look, I'm just not smart enough to get this new procedure," a helpful reframe might be "I have seen you tackle difficult problems like this in the past. I know you can do it. Let's work together on this."

Develop positive affirmations. Help the employee identify their top strengths and opportunities, in order to reinforce realistic thinking and understanding of their competencies. Help them feel good about what they do well and find a path for professional development.

> **Example:** "I know you are one of the best pickers in the warehouse, and now I'd like to be sure you learn the fundamentals of our shipping procedures."

Be vulnerable. It is okay to let them know you are worried or concerned. Employees can argue about the facts and circumstances, but they can't argue with how you feel. It is a strength to use your own emotional experience to help move them to new patterns of behavior. Vulnerability, typically framed as a weakness, is actually a very potent motivator of human behavior. It can be a powerful pivot point, a place where people make the unconsciously virtuous decision to lean in and help.

> **Example:** "Sam, I feel worried that your claim of helplessness is getting in the way of what I know you want to accomplish. It feels to me like you are stuck— and that is not a strength for anyone." One advantage of this approach is that there are no "facts" to refute; Sam can't reply, "No, you're not worried . . ." The focus here is the manager's concern for his staff member and getting Sam to respond to the worry rather than react defensively to the feedback.

Victim Mentality

In this mentality, the employee believes they are the victim of the negative intentions and actions of others, even in the absence of evidence. People with this attitude will blame others or be unwilling to take responsibility for a situation they've created or contributed to.

What You Need to Do

When working with an employee who has the victim attitude, consider these approaches:

Label the mindset. This should not be done in a belittling or shaming way. Keep your demeanor neutral to positive, and show some understanding and empathy about the situation (not their victim frame). A neutral identification of their mindset is enough to help someone better understand their behavior.

> **Example:** "Kevin, sometimes it feels to me like you see yourself as a victim—and I just have never thought of you as helpless or the target of some kind of campaign to undermine your success."

Identify the consequences of the victim attitude. Some people are motivated to act like a victim, as odd as that sounds. People behave in certain ways, even negative ways, in large part because of the payoff they imagine (often unconsciously). Let's look at a few of the typical payoffs for the "victim":

- I get attention.

- I avoid personal responsibility/accountability.

- I feel justified or right.

- I have a sense of being guilt-free.

- I am treated unfairly, so you should feel sorry for me.

These perceived payoffs need to be countered with higher-value consequences. Help the employee see how much the victim mentality costs them, especially relationally.

> **Example:** "Bethany, I am worried that your 'I am a victim' attitude is pushing people away from you. You seem less integrated with the team, and people are beginning to think they can't count on you. This is causing you to be labeled as someone who is unreliable, and I know you are capable of so much more."

Focus on the team and its mission. Help the employee refocus on the bigger picture, not just think of themselves. Ask them if they could imagine thinking just as much (or more) about the "we" instead of the "me."

> **Example:** "I need you to expand your understanding of what it takes for us to be successful as a team. We need a team player right now as we work out this issue. We can't afford to have you simply shut down in defeat. People are counting on you."

Take advantage of growth opportunities. Often "victims" struggle or become more negative when they face difficult challenges. Helping them develop a strong sense of perseverance in the face of challenge is a key way to help them overcome a victim mentality. To increase resiliency, it is important to surround that team member with support, whether that means coming alongside them or connecting them with a mentor or workplace partner so that they feel more confident facing obstacles head on.

> **Example:** "Sarah, I know this feels really hard when you don't feel supported by Ken. I know it hasn't always been easy. I do appreciate that you have continued to

> collaborate with him to complete the project. This has made a real difference for our team. Your positive 'can do' attitude will be critical to finishing this project successfully. Now, how can I better support you?"

Be solution focused. Work with the employee to map out potential solutions. This helps to establish a positive frame around how to move forward. Tell them you need their help to do so.

> **Example:** "Anyone can be problem focused; there is nothing impressive there. I need someone who can help me come up with some potential solutions—that takes grit and commitment to the team and the company. Can I count on you to help me with this? You always bring great ideas to the table, and I could really use your input."

Grudge Collectors

Grudge collecting is a common personality trait where employees see neutral or even positive actions as additional "evidence" that the organization and its leaders want to do them harm. In one company we worked with, the CEO responded to employee frustrations about outdated maps in their service vehicles by installing state-of-the-art GPS technology in every truck. Response from the grudge collectors? "Now they are tracking us!"

What You Need to Do

When working with an employee who has a grudge collector attitude, consider these approaches:

Identify the issues. Grudge collectors wear attitudinal blinders that prevent them from seeing the positive motivations and actions of others, particularly management. They will shake their head in denial of their negative, one-dimensional view of the organization and its leaders and will label those who disagree with them as naive and dumb. They usually are passive-aggressive, smiling at leaders in the moment and then trashing them later in conversations with peers. Grudge collectors promote their cynicism with others, creating a contagion of negativity as they undermine core values and sow disengagement among those they infect.

One of the best ways to prevent these grudges from building up and going viral is to allow employees the opportunity to discuss their distress. You can do this by holding regular meetings for the sole purpose of addressing employees' concerns. This gives the grudge collectors an opportunity to express their opinion, and allows you as the manager to mitigate the effects of the given problem(s) before they take hold.

Encourage self-awareness. Similar to the victim mentality, the grudge-collecting mentality must also be labeled. The employee might not even be aware of their negative mentality or how it's affecting them and others. It's important to address this issue in a constructive, nonthreatening way that won't cause your employee to become defensive.

> **Example:** "Lisa, you're a valued employee here, and that is why I'm concerned that something's causing you to have a negative mindset. Can we talk about

what's causing you to complain so often? If there are some changes we need to make I'd like your help."

Show gratitude. Unfortunately, negativity comes naturally to grudge collectors and has a tendency to grow over time. Having these individuals focus on something positive can help balance out their negative dispositions. Encourage them to jot down three things each morning that they are grateful for before they start their workday. Making this practice of expressing their gratitude a daily habit will increase a positive mindset. Check in within a week to see how they are doing. If they have expressed gratitude about someone on the team, encourage them to write a thank-you note or email to that team member.

Organizational Obstacles

Organizations, like people, can develop institutional habits that get in the way, that discourage accountability engagement—the desire or motivation for staff to be responsible. If left uncorrected long enough, these organizational bad habits become embedded in the culture. Typical examples would include unclear or competing priorities ("Am I working on the right thing?"), a silo mentality ("We need to take care of our needs first."), and conflict avoidance ("It will work itself out eventually. I'm too busy to deal with that now.").

Unclear or Competing Priorities

A lack of clarity around expectations and priorities corrodes accountability. This may sound too simple, but it is important for individuals to know what they are accountable for. Without clarity, employees can be accountable to the wrong goals, or hold back discretionary effort as a result of confusion and uncertainty. This decline in accountability happens not necessarily from a lack of commitment but rather because employees do not have a clear picture of what they are supposed to do. Accountability suffers when desired tasks and behaviors are not clearly established.

What You Need to Do

When you think there is a lack of clarity around priorities, consider these approaches:

Agree on outcomes. Managers should establish expectations around outcomes collaboratively. When team members determine outcomes together, they have a better understanding of the context and meaning behind specific words or targets. When they are part of the process, they know the "why" behind the task, and this can significantly increase their commitment to getting the job done.

Agree on behaviors. Organizations are typically pretty good at setting goals and outcomes (although not always in a collaborative way), but there is often significant opportunity to increase accountability around behavioral expectations—how individuals and teams show up and complete tasks.

> **Example:** "Okay, we have agreed on what we need to accomplish over the next three weeks. The only way we will be able to complete this effectively is if we all collaborate closely with other members of the team. We need to work together, respect our individual skill sets, and share our progress on a daily basis. I'm

setting aside the last twenty minutes of each day for a team huddle so we can all compare notes."

Agree on metrics. We know that performance metrics increase employee engagement, and so it goes for accountability. "A" players appreciate metrics, in part because the detailed information validates their engaged behavior—there is clear data that they not only meet but exceed expectations. Managers should seek agreement on appropriate metrics with the team, collaboratively and inclusively.

Agree to collaborate. Decisions made by individuals without input from the rest of the team can lead to a number of negative outcomes. Problems such as unrealistic expectations (both high and low), delays and redos, or lack of buy-in, can easily arise if stakeholders are left out of the decision-making process. Isolated decisions also cause team members to second-guess themselves or reduce risk taking, because they know the leader will just take over the decision process anyway. This can be extremely corrosive to individual performance and the broader workplace culture.

Agree on timing. This is a very straightforward need but one often overlooked. Managers often establish what the deadline is for a project, but they typically overlook the opportunity to establish interim milestones. This is a great way for employees to pace themselves in order to avoid a compression of activity (which increases mistakes and stress and reduces mental acuity) in the days just before the deadline. Managers should check in at each milestone to ensure team members are staying current on task execution and to determine any additional needs, support, or concerns the team may have and make adjustments as necessary.

Agree on other performance standards. Depending on the nature of the work, there may be other performance standards that are important to establish as a group or team. These might include:

- *Quality standards:* Are we clear on what factors need to be in place for a high-quality product or service?

- *Cost standards:* What are the budget constraints for the task?

- *Quantity standards:* How many products need to be produced each day, each week, each month?

- *Scrap standards:* Does the team care about levels of scrap and waste associated with meeting the goals?

- *Work-life balance standards:* How important is it to the team that the balance between task accomplishment and a healthy personal life be maintained?

Silo Mentality

Functional areas (e.g., accounting, marketing) and individual teams can become insular and defensive toward other groups in the organization. When this happens, the free flow of information chokes, unhealthy competition can develop, and a "we vs. them" mentality can contribute to conditions and behaviors antithetical to accountability.

What You Need to Do

When you think there is a lack of communication among teams or departments, consider these approaches:

Encourage interdepartmental communication. This "we vs. them" mentality is most likely to occur when teams don't know each other well, especially if they've never actually interacted in person. In a way, the inability to put a face to a name dehumanizes the nature of the relationship. Think about it—when you're talking to a telemarketer, are you more or less likely to be polite than when you're having a face-to-face conversation? As herd animals, hardwired to connect with others, we work best with those we have an established relationship with. Leaders should foster opportunities for employees to connect with other teams through cross-departmental collaboration, as well as in informal and social settings.

Define the root of the problem. This one may seem obvious, but you'd be amazed at how often it's overlooked. Without identifying the issue, it's nearly impossible to address it. Often, the problem might be that the groups have conflicting priorities. In this case, you can hold employees accountable by explaining how their actions or attitudes are affecting the other group.

Identify common interests. What is the bigger picture? At a higher altitude, what is the team trying to achieve? The higher the altitude the discussion begins, the easier it is to establish common values and reach consensus. Start at the top—shared values, for example—and then work your way down to the more granular details of the presumed conflict. This process often establishes context and meaning that helps the parties find resolution.

> **Example:** "First, I want to thank each department represented here. We came together three months ago to better coordinate our efforts for improving our customer's experience. We all agreed on the need to increase both our repeat business and customer referrals. Is that still how we all see the primary objective? Are we all in agreement on that as one of our original outcomes?"

Starting at this altitude allows the discussion leader to begin the conversation with where the interests of the different departments overlap and intersect. A good facilitator will then drop in altitude incrementally, trying to maintain consensus. When discussion participants begin with consensus, they are far more likely to end there.

Conflict Avoidance

When superficial harmony is valued more than true consensus, authentic responsibility suffers. One of the key reasons the actively disengaged get so much traction in company cultures is that engaged employees do not hold them accountable in the everyday conversations where the disengaged tend to spread their toxicity. Because holding someone accountable has traditionally been seen and felt as conflictual, good employees avoid the corrective, "tough" conversation with their negative colleague—largely out of conflict avoidance.

What You Need to Do

When you think there is a lack of candor among staff, consider these approaches:

Practice open and honest communication framed by core values. When this kind of communication is practiced regularly, it becomes the norm—whether in positive interactions or difficult ones. To facilitate open dialogue about the connection between organizational core values and the behaviors and attitudes of employees, managers need to model and encourage regular collaboration. With time, employees will become more comfortable with a values-framed conversation in order to more easily and effectively hold others accountable.

Establish discussion norms. Develop a set of expectations about how discussions will transpire. What behavioral norms are participants expected to follow? Whenever possible, link these characteristics to core values. Potential norms might include:

- *Mutual respect:* People's word choices, voice tone, and body language should remain professional.

- *Using "I" statements:* Say, for example, "I believe the most important issue is . . ." instead of "The most important issue is . . ." The goal is to convey that there may be other viewpoints or facts the speaker is not aware of, so speaking in "I" statements offers a "here is what I know" perspective. Using "I" statements in this way helps avoid the frame "I am the last word. You better just do what I say."

□ *No interruptions*: Everyone deserves to be heard without being interrupted.

□ *No filibusters*: People don't get to talk forever—they should be encouraged to state their points briefly and concisely.

□ *Mutual benefit*: Keep the discussion focused on what is better for the team, for the most effective outcome.

□ *No blaming or finger pointing*: Keep the discussion focused on process, new best practices, continuous improvement, solutions, etc.

□ *Mutual agreement*: The discussion leader should seek mutual agreement incrementally as points are discussed and then again at the end regarding what the action steps are going forward.

While these points are framed for meetings and more formal settings, they also apply to informal conversations, such as impromptu exchanges in the break room and the hallway. All of the interactions between employees should be held to the same positively framed, high standard.

HOW TO APPLY ACCOUNTABILITY

Trust is the outcome of a felt sense of safety. People perform at their best when they feel safe (e.g., they have safe and secure connections in an environment that is both predictable and consistent). Building trust only happens when people are in an environment the brain considers trustworthy. A manager who only periodically holds employees accountable is not likely to be seen by others as trustworthy. The critical ingredient is not accountability per se—it is the consistent, predictable demonstration of what we call accountability principles. Because we are prosocial animals at our core, being among others who are consistently accountable not only contributes to a felt sense of safety, it also encourages similar behaviors in ourselves and others.

Let's look at a few accountability principles.

Intention

Employees who begin their day intending specific accomplishments (finish the market study, clean up the warehouse) or behaviors (be supportive, collaborative, forgiving) are much more likely to carry them out. How can you help your team members be more intentional when they start the day?

Personal Integrity

In organizations, integrity is seen as doing the right thing, even when difficult or inconvenient, even when no one is looking. It's doing what you say you'll do and being fair and impartial as you do it. When someone accepts the consequences of performance shortfalls and works to fix them, for example, we would say they are a person of integrity—they are accountable.

Part of the definition of integrity also includes *having strong moral principles*. The way leaders lead their lives does matter. People lacking *moral* uprightness might say, "My personal life is irrelevant at work," but their personal life does matter. It speaks directly to the character and integrity of the leader, regardless of their rank and title. As a manager, do you think your staff would call you a person of integrity?

Core Values Integrity

Just as individuals need to stay true to their words, organizations need to follow through on their core principles. Upholding core values is primarily in the hands of managers, since they have the most frequent interactions and (hopefully) the most trusted relationship with each of their team members. Senior leaders need to promote congruence to organizational core values, but their lofty words fall on deaf ears if their actions don't correlate with what employees experience on the job. Nowhere is alignment with values more important than in the daily deportment of a manager. The ways in which managers live and enforce enterprise principles is critical. One of the hardest things for leadership to do, based on my experience with clients, is to fire someone who is very productive and task focused but who is behaviorally or attitudinally misaligned. When the manager eventually fires the troubling staff member, employees typically say things like "What took you so long?" or "It's about time." What they are really saying is something like this: "We've been waiting for you to step up like a true leader and protect us. Where have you been?" Few things undermine a leader's street cred more quickly than a reluctance, resistance, or vacillation toward upholding the organization's core values.

Competence

Are you capable of doing what you say you will? Do you realistically assess what you can do, both in terms of time and ability? Do you make commitments you can't keep? Good managers rely on their strengths and focus on their opportunities. To increase your competence, learn what your strengths are and lean on them. Continue learning to expand your capabilities.

Follow-Through

Do you finish the job and check in with all the stakeholders? Do you communicate and celebrate? Can others count on you to do everything you said you would do, and do you check in with them to make sure that standards have been met?

Meeting Expectations

When things go as expected and we deliver predictable outcomes, we build credibility that makes us more trustworthy. When things don't go as expected, taking personal accountability builds credibility and trustworthiness, especially if the team goals include collecting "lessons learned."

Profiting from Mistakes

One of the best ways to embrace mistakes, regardless of who or what is at fault, is to focus on how to do it more effectively next time. Identify new or better best practices, and frame the discussion as constructive feedback, not constructive criticism (a condition that does not exist in the brain). Keep the blame at bay. Assigning blame never enhances one's character or trustworthiness.

Seeking Feedback

The desire to get better at what you do at work is an important part of personal accountability, regardless of rank or title. Continuous improvement applies to leaders at all levels as well as employees in nonmanagerial positions. Do you seek feedback from your direct reports on how you are doing? Do you ask them what else you could do to enable them to be more successful?

In this chapter, I wanted to offer a new, more actionable view of accountability. It is more than simply acting responsibly—it is being accountable to a standard or value that motivates behavioral change in organizationally beneficial directions. Leaders at all levels can use these common obstacles, suggested remedies, and approaches promoting consistent accountability to significantly strengthen their leadership competence. Managers who hold high standards for themselves that are both rigorous and relational, and who help others to do the same, will have teams that are more accountable, where individuals perform closer to their full capacity—even when no one is looking.

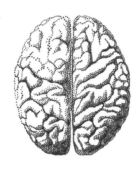

CHAPTER INSIGHTS

➤ Accountability is critical for a safe, thriving work environment. Without it, your high performers can become discouraged and leave as your low performers persist in their negative or unaccountable behaviors—undermining organizational performance and your status as an effective leader.

➤ There are a number of ways individuals can demonstrate obstacles to accountability. Three of the most common are learned helplessness, a victim mentality, and grudge collecting.

⤳ To effectively address *individual* obstacles to accountability, leaders can employ a variety of behaviors such as active listening, showing curiosity, expressing vulnerability, and encouraging employees to get involved in the solution to the problem.

⤳ Organizational obstacles, such as unclear priorities, silos, and conflict avoidance, can easily corrode accountability.

⤳ To effectively address *organizational* obstacles to accountability, leaders can focus on more inclusive decision making, agreeing on outcomes and priorities as a group, and ensuring open, clear communication organization-wide.

⤳ Accountable managers lead by example. They demonstrate integrity, follow-through, competence, and openness to feedback.

CHAPTER ACTION STEPS

⤳ *Reflect:* How can I strengthen the accountability of my team or organization? Are there particular employees I need to hold more accountable? Am I allowing organizational obstacles to get in the way of achieving our goals?

⤳ *Act:* Take time to regularly review your employees' performance with them personally. The more consistent your communication with each direct report, the less you will have to confront big accountability issues. Ask questions instead of pointing fingers and find ways to equip unaccountable employees and teams with the necessary resources and training to succeed.

↪ *For Manager Resource Center subscribers:* Visit ManagerResourceCenter.com and download **Holding Others Accountable Without Being Negative** from your toolkit. Learn how to create and maintain a culture of accountability without being punitive or coddling.

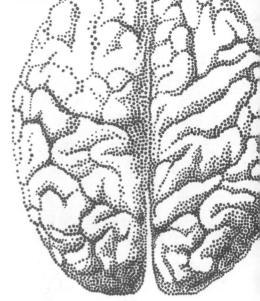

<u>C H A P T E R 9</u>

YOU CAN'T MANAGE WHAT YOU DON'T MEASURE

It is a capital mistake to theorize before one has data.[80]
—SHERLOCK HOLMES

Why measure employee engagement? There are several reasons that top the list for me. First, the things you measure get noticed. Talking about the importance of a high-performance workplace will get nods of approval. Measuring the details of what increases engagement for every team, department, and physical location will get action from those leaders in charge.

Second, collecting data using a survey provides clarity for managers at every level in the company regarding what is expected of them. Managers are overwhelmed with tasks; leading has never been so complex. A good survey is not just an assessment tool; it should also provide a laundry list of what leaders need to do to influence real culture shifts across the enterprise. It should make the necessary

---

80 Arthur Conan Doyle, *A Study in Scarlet* (Filiquarian, 2007).

changes easier, less obscure, and more actionable. Questions should be based on drivers of behavioral change, not popularity scores for how "satisfied" employees are.

Third—and this may seem a little strange—almost anything you measure with rigor and regularity improves. Of course, having the right questions helps. Measuring can have this impact primarily because it leads people to be more intentional and focused as a result of what is being evaluated. Think about it this way: If you are in the habit of stepping on the scale regularly, you are more aware of and attuned to what your body needs and how it's impacted by the food and exercise choices you make. You have a clearer picture of where you stand and what you are doing that causes the scale to move up or down when you track your weight regularly—and you are more likely to make choices that encourage a healthy lifestyle. The same is true for tracking engagement with regularity—once a year is sufficient as long as timely and consistent actions are taken in response to the results. More on that in chapter 10.

The point here is something we have seen with every client—metrics give employee engagement initiatives an energy and effectiveness boost. Leaders at all levels in the organization get more engaged and focused, and because the survey (and associated communication from senior leaders) touches every employee, the entire enterprise becomes more conscious of both the intent and the substance of the program.

When CEOs want to improve employee engagement in their organizations, the first step I recommend is to measure employees' engagement levels. This singular act sends a message to the entire organization that the focus on engagement is serious and long term. One manager came up to me at the end of a workshop looking a little worried and said, "I guess they are really serious about this engagement stuff if they are going to survey the entire company." "Exactly," I replied, "and that is why learning these new leadership skills is so important for you."

To properly manage employee engagement, you have to collect data, which then allows the conversation to be more substantive and strategic so that leaders can pinpoint where actions are needed. Surveying also establishes what is possible and helps eliminate excuses. During a survey debrief I conducted with a team leader, she looked at her results and frowned. "It's impossible to get higher scores with all we are expected to do," she said defensively. "You are right, the demands are high," I replied, "but there are ten workgroups in the company where employees are 100 percent engaged, so we know it *can* be done. Let's take a deeper look at your data and make a plan."

Using a survey year over year delivers data trends that allow leaders to see what's improving and where they need more work. It can help reveal which managers have improved and who is still struggling, which means senior leaders can identify which managers need validation for a job well done, and which need help getting to the next level.

Without data to back up a strategic initiative focused on culture and leader behaviors, conviction and enthusiasm can dwindle. Here is a typical approach based on multiple stories I have heard from CEOs: The leadership team decides it wants to focus on employee engagement and rolls out some programs focused on culture, mission, and vision. Managers might get new training and focus on a new set of KPIs. A year later, the team gets back together to talk about how things have changed—but without any data to benchmark progress, the conversation feels anecdotal. Some aren't sure the programs ever got traction, and the team members who never liked the approach jump on the chance to disparage the entire initiative.

WHAT TO LOOK FOR IN A SURVEY TOOL

Selecting the right survey tool is an essential first step, and there are many survey options on the market. As you consider the different approaches for measuring employee engagement, there are three things to avoid.

First, make sure you are not looking at an employee *satisfaction* survey. Employee satisfaction is not the same as employee engagement. In an employee satisfaction survey, you are primarily measuring employees' attitudes. When you measure employee *engagement*, you are assessing behaviors. Here is how researchers describe the difference: "Engagement connotes activation, whereas satisfaction connotes satiation. In addition, although 'satisfaction' surveys that ask employees to describe their work conditions may be relevant for assessing the conditions that *provide for* engagement, they do not directly tap engagement."[81] Attitudes can fluctuate with one negative or positive event, and regularly asking employees how happy they are will simply increase a sense of entitlement and the perception that the role of management is to keep employees happy. That is not the role of management! Also, an employee can be satisfied at work but still not be able to identify meaning and purpose in what they do, and they might not be aligned with mission, vision, and values.

We know that if employees are engaged, their actions are more predictable, productive, and positive. The role of leadership is to provide an environment where employees can be engaged, and when that is accomplished, employees are not only satisfied but also strong contributors to the organization.

Second, avoid surveys that are excessively long. The proprietary survey we use at E3 has only twenty-eight questions. We have discov-

---

81   William H. Macey and Benjamin Schneider, "The Meaning of Employee Engagement," *Industrial and Organizational Psychology* 1, no. 1 (2008): 8.

ered that employees begin suffering from survey fatigue after about thirty questions. Select a survey that is no longer than thirty-five questions to increase your chances of employees participating. The last thing you want is the early respondents starting a narrative like "Oh my gosh, it took *forever*" or giving up on thoughtful answers altogether just to get to the end of the survey.

Finally, keep a watchful eye out for questions similar to "Do you think you are paid a fair and equitable wage?" This is an important question, but it should not be asked in an engagement survey. Employees tend to bias their answer on this question negatively, and when the survey results indicate, for example, that "65 percent of employees do not feel they are paid fairly," there is an expectation that everyone will get a raise. And when that raise doesn't happen, employees will view the entire engagement initiative as ineffective because they won't feel heard. Assuming staff are paid fairly, the compensation question overemphasizes the role of money as a driver of high performance and reinforces perceptions that employee disengagement can only be "fixed" by paying people more. Additionally, when people are miserable at work, they are less likely to feel fairly compensated. You've heard the old phrase "You couldn't pay me enough to work there." We see it in our data. When asked why they like coming to work, the most disengaged employees in an organization say, "a paycheck," and when asked what would increase engagement levels, they say, "Pay me more." When the most engaged staff are asked why they like coming to work, we commonly see answers like "feels like family," "I'm challenged every day," "I work with great people." The highly engaged are rarely focused on the money; the disengaged see little else.

The primary issue regarding pay is making sure that employees are paid a fair and equitable wage. Beyond that, pay levels pale in comparison to other behavioral drivers.[82] If business owners pay women less than men, for example, don't be surprised if female employees are somewhat disengaged. It is a natural response to a dysfunctional business practice. When employees are not paid a fair and equitable wage, it's almost impossible to get any discretionary effort and sustainable engagement. It is helpful for leaders to understand employee perceptions about pay fairness; just don't ask the question in your employee engagement survey. Do it another time—in focus groups or in a smaller, spot survey.

Now that I have said what you should avoid, let me focus on what you should be looking for. Here are the basics:

1. Be brief, no more than thirty-five questions (under thirty is even better).

2. Include science-based questions on relational drivers of human behavior—the things the brain needs for safe and secure attachments (trusted social resources).

3. Find a survey that provides managers with some clarity about what the organization thinks great leaders should be doing. The goal is not simply to assess—it is to lead.

In addition to these basics, I see three foundational elements for effectively moving an organization toward higher levels of performance and engagement. First, leaders and employees need to *envision* the company and culture they want; people move more purposefully when they know where they are going and why. Second, leaders need to be *empowered* with science-based skills to help them create the conditions where employees will thrive. Managers tell us regularly that they want to get off the latest leadership fad approach and lock in

---

82 Alfie Kohn, *Punished by Rewards: The Trouble with Gold Stars, Incentive Plans, A's, Praise, and Other Bribes,* (New York: Houghton Mifflin, 1999).

on a more substantive path toward improving their leadership skills. Third, fortified with directional clarity and proven pro-engagement tools, managers and other leaders can *engage* with staff in ways that elicit improved performance and positivity across a broad range of desired outcomes.

E3 Solution's assessment tool, the E3A, is a research-driven, online diagnostic tool that helps CEOs and other senior leaders get a clear and accurate picture of their organization's engagement levels. It measures the quality of the relationships between leaders at all levels and the employees who report to them. It can identify critical shortfalls in performance, behaviors, and productivity well before customers feel an impact. The E3A identifies opportunities by region, division, team, and manager; provides additional insight based on tenure, age, and gender cohort; and delivers detailed, forward-looking indicators for critical business metrics like productivity, profitability, and the customer experience.

The survey results deliver a uniquely accurate picture of the organization's strengths and key opportunities, identifying broad themes and determining within each individual team what is going well, what is holding steady, and what needs improvement.

The tool consists of twenty-eight hard-coded survey questions based on what we know drives engagement, aggregated into three areas, or "leadership dimensions": *Focus, Capability,* and *Mindset.* Our survey also includes three to five client-selected, open-ended questions allowing employees to speak more specifically about their workplace experience. Their responses to these questions are often detailed and, from our experience, provide some of the most telling (and compelling) challenges facing senior leaders.

Many executives have what can only be characterized as an emotional experience after reviewing this feedback. "I love the data," one client CEO told me recently, "but hearing the actual voices of my employees in their written answers to these questions is incredibly valuable." It brings a remarkable amount of transparency about the employee-to-manager relationship in a workplace culture. Because these responses are anonymous and cannot be tied to any single respondent, employees can offer their input in a safe and productive manner, without fear of negative repercussions if they have something difficult or uncomfortable to share. Employees want their voices heard (both in the data and the open-ended questions), but they don't want to be identified. Employee anonymity is critical in establishing trust in the tool. This is a key reason why companies should not run an engagement survey themselves.

The output of the E3A is reliable, pragmatic, and actionable, based on direct, unfiltered feedback from employees at every level of the organization. By identifying and prioritizing the proven drivers of engaged behavior, senior leaders can work more effectively with individual managers and supervisors in setting priorities for improvement.

FOUR LEVELS OF ENGAGEMENT

We divide engagement into four levels:

1. The actively disengaged

2. The somewhat disengaged

3. The engaged

4. The actively engaged

We use a bell curve to represent these engagement levels.

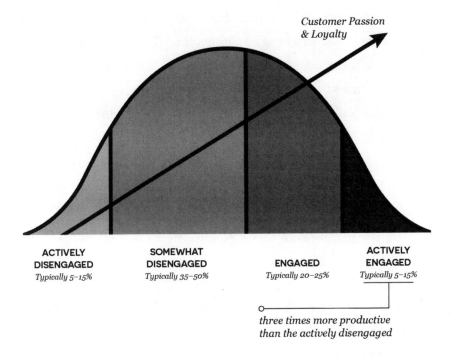

ACTIVELY DISENGAGED	SOMEWHAT DISENGAGED	ENGAGED	ACTIVELY ENGAGED
Typically 5–15%	*Typically 35–50%*	*Typically 20–25%*	*Typically 5–15%*

*three times more productive
than the actively disengaged*

It is helpful to visualize a bell curve when measuring employee engagement. E3 Solutions divides the curve into four categories. The negative deviants on the left (the actively disengaged) typically comprise 5 to 15 percent of employees and the somewhat disengaged (typically the largest group when measuring for the first time), typically range from 35 to 50 percent. We separate the engaged employees (around 20 to 25 percent of staff) from the actively engaged on the right side of the bell curve (about 5 to 15 percent of employees) to reflect the high-energy, focused intensity of "A" players over other employees. The high water mark for our most successful clients is having 74 percent of their staff engaged (combining the engaged and actively engaged employees).

Looking on the left side of the bell curve, we can see the negative outliers. These **actively disengaged** employees are the 5–15 percent who have essentially quit—but forgot to tell you! They still show up and collect a paycheck, but they do the bare minimum amount of work, just enough to keep from getting pulled aside or fired. They may be in attendance for eight hours, but they're only giving the company about four hours of real work.

Moving toward the center of the bell curve, the next category is the **somewhat disengaged** employees. This group is typically the largest, representing 35–50 percent of the employees. These employees may be occasionally engaged, but they clearly are not functioning at or near their full potential. The productivity of the individuals in this group is a little better than the actively disengaged; out of eight hours, they're putting in about five and a quarter hours of work during the day.

Crossing the threshold to engagement on the right-hand side, we find the truly **engaged** employees. This group represents 20–35 percent of employees in a typical company; they're putting in an honest day's labor for a full day's pay. These employees are the salt of the earth—they work hard, they are more likely to believe in the company's mission and vision, and their outlook tends to be more positive in everything they do.

The extremely positive outliers on the far right are what we call the **actively engaged** employees, representing 5–15 percent of workers in typical organizations. These employees are reliably hyper-productive, giving close to one and one-half day's work for a full day's pay. They are internal and external ambassadors for the brand, and they believe in and work in congruence with the organization's core values. They are far more likely to feel fulfilled by, connected with, and faithful to the company, their team, and their leader.

Many of our E3A clients come to us because of the hemorrhaging of productivity, negativity, and wasted payroll occurring on the left side of the bell curve. It's been estimated that 25 percent of most organizations' spending on human resources and benefits are wasted due to the subpar performance of disengaged employees. We already outlined a broad array of additional costs in chapter 5.

Understanding the level of loss is always eye opening, and one of the primary benefits of the E3A is the clarity it offers on where remedies are needed. Organizations want to know where to focus their efforts to improve engagement, and the data from our survey tool provides a wealth of insight to that end. Looking at the comparative workgroup data—indicating which managers are struggling—combined with a deeper dive into the rank-ordered twenty-eight questions—gives leadership remarkable clarity on what steps need to be taken and where.

LEADERSHIP DIMENSIONS

As I mentioned previously, we aggregate the questions into three leadership dimensions: *focus, capability,* and *mindset.*

Focus allows employees to channel their efforts and reduces the distractions that dilute their performance. Managers and other leaders must ensure that employees are focused on the most important tasks and that they support and encourage conditions that increase focus—like clear directions, the ability to ask questions, and transparent and two-way communication. It also helps when staff has a firm understanding of the organization's mission and vision. Six of the questions in the survey roll up into a combined score on *focus* to highlight employees' clarity around expectations, their immediate tasks, where the organization is headed, and their role in facilitating the organization's success.

The second dimension, *capability*, assesses whether employees believe they have the necessary tools, resources, training, and collaboration to get their job done. When team members are able to use their strengths daily and they feel supported by their team, engagement increases. *Capability* also means they are not inhibited by dysfunctional or unfair processes within the organization. Seven of our survey questions provide this score.

The third leadership dimension is *mindset*. Having the right mindset or attitude is essential for any employee to maximize his or her value to the organization. This is one of the most challenging areas for management: What can be done to improve morale, commitment to the organization, or accountability? This gets to the heart of the issue of discretionary effort. Employees must want to do a good job, and they must have the will to perform at their best. There are many factors that impact an employee's mindset, such as trust, collaboration, a felt sense of safety, a relational (versus transactional) culture, fairness, meaning, and purpose. This is about the quality of relationships employees have with their manager and their colleagues, the levels of trust they have with their colleagues, whether their opinions count, and whether they're valued for more than the work they produce. Leaders who encourage these conditions will have more effective teams and more engaged employees overall. Because mindset is critical to an employee's engagement level in the organization, half the questions (fifteen) in our survey contribute to the *mindset* score.

A CENSUS SURVEY

The E3 team works with clients to get as close to 100 percent participation in the survey as possible. Our clients have achieved as high as 98 percent participation, making the survey more of a census than a poll. The very action of taking the survey actually starts the process of increasing engagement, which is why we stress the importance of high participation rates.

For many employees, this survey tool is the first time they've been asked their opinion on issues related to leadership quality and the company's well-being, and the very fact that leaders in the organization are deploying a survey tool like this sends a message that they want to know how things are going. That fact alone increases engagement.

As you can see, I am a strong believer in measuring. This is in part because I have seen the outcome in companies once they begin this process. Every one of our survey clients has seen significant improvements year over year. But administering a survey is just the first step in the process—what senior leaders do with the data is critical for success. In the next chapter, we will lay out how remarkably powerful the data can be when used effectively.

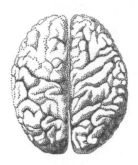

CHAPTER INSIGHTS

↪ Metrics boost the commitment to employee engagement initiatives within an organization as well as their clarity and effectiveness.

↪ Three things you should look for in a survey tool: (1) it measures engagement, not satisfaction, (2) it is no longer than thirty to thirty-five questions, (3) it asks the right kind of questions, which truly correlate to conditions that create engagement in an organization.

➡ There are four types of employees in every organization. The *actively disengaged* are the employees who quit but forgot to tell you and are still getting paid. *Somewhat disengaged* employees are ambivalent about their commitment to the company, their peers, and customers. *Engaged* employees show up in a positive frame of mind and put in a decent day's work. *Actively engaged* employees—your highest performers—are rock stars when it comes to productivity, integrity, commitment, and alignment with company core values, mission, and vision.

➡ We identify three leadership dimensions useful in examining employees' engagement level in the organization. *Focus* allows employees to have clear direction and understanding of their job role and how it fits in with the organization's mission. *Capability* determines whether an employee has all the resources, tools, and training necessary to do their job effectively. *Mindset* is about the state of mind or attitude of an employee, and it improves when they have healthy connections with their manager and their colleagues. When employees have a positive mindset (resulting from feeling valued, strong collaboration, and a felt sense of safety), clear focus, and the tools and training enabling full capability, they are more likely to be highly engaged in the organization.

CHAPTER ACTION STEPS

➡ *Reflect:* What can I do to provide more focus to my team? Have I done all I can to be sure they have the tools and training to perform at their best? How can I improve the quality of the relationships of my team with me, with each other, and with additional key players in the organization?

➡ *Act:* Use a simple (and free) online survey platform like SurveyGizmo or Google Forms to poll your team for anonymous answers. Ask questions like: What is our most important mission as a team? How does our work as a team fit in with the big picture for our organization? What additional tools or training would allow you to perform better at your job? How can I better support your success? Review the answers and look for opportunities to fill gaps and to be responsive. Alternatively, contact E3 Solutions to use our twenty-eight question survey for immediate insights on employee engagement levels.

➡ *For Manager Resource Center subscribers:* Visit ManagerResourceCenter.com and download **How to Conduct a K.I.S.S Exercise**. Use the instructions to crowdsource what changes can be focused on right away in your organization.

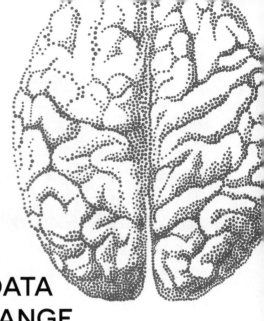

CHAPTER 10

MOVING FROM DATA TO CULTURE CHANGE

The goal is to turn data into information,
and information into insight.

—CARLY FIORINA

I received a call from John, a CEO I met at a Vistage meeting recently.[83] He was struggling with his data from a popular workplace satisfaction survey that tries to determine how well liked a company is among its employees. His numbers were essentially the same as in the previous two years, and he wasn't sure what to do next. "I get all these numbers," he said, "but not a lot of guidance on what to do to improve." I have heard this dozens of times from other CEOs who find their interest in the process beginning to wane when survey numbers don't move (or when they move down).

Leaders can feel overwhelmed with the mountain of data that results from a rigorous survey. It is easy to get lost in the standard points

---

83 Vistage (www.vistage.com) is the largest CEO membership organization in the world. Don Rheem has spoken to more than five hundred Vistage groups in the United States, Canada, and Great Britain.

of deviation, variances, and cross tabs. As we said in the previous chapter, you can't manage what you don't measure. By the same token, data collection is not change management. Changing behaviors is a limbic system issue. Employees need to pivot from the old motivations for underperformance to new ones promoting performance excellence.

Managing change, the process of encouraging more engaged, prosocial, and productive behaviors, is enormously difficult. Most change management initiatives are unsuccessful in fully reaching their initial objectives, because their focus is almost exclusively tactical: what needs to be done, who is in charge, and what is the deadline? The project leads create complex matrixed diagrams that make everything look very systematized. However, it takes a lot more than logic and efficient processes to change human behavior. Processes and procedures can help if they are seen as fair, collaborative, and transparent, but that isn't enough (and they rarely embody all three).

Changing behavior is more about emotion than logic or process. Most change is perceived as a potential threat to the limbic system, so there are hardwired, often silent, voices telling us to beware, to be cautious—maybe even to distrust and resist. In short, the felt experience of change, especially when it is mandated, unanticipated, and poorly explained, is usually negative, and the commensurate behaviors are both predictable and typically unsupportive.

The point in measuring is to use meaningful data to improve performance. Leaders need help making better decisions to resolve root issues that interfere with performance excellence. Every one of our survey clients has shown improvement year-over-year, in some cases quite remarkably.[84] But intentional leaders best maximize this improvement

---

84 There is one exception—when companies hit employee engagement levels of 65–74 percent (our highest level when combining the *engaged* and *actively engaged* categories), their YOY results can fluctuate within a few percentage points. This may represent a true top end for employee engagement results based on what we measure or on what is

by using the data to create effective shifts during the intervals between the surveys, rather than simply relying on the survey process itself.

CEOs use employee engagement data most effectively when they establish a baseline (the results from the first survey), set goals for improvement, and give managers better science-based skills to achieve them. They then measure again (in nine to twelve months) to track and celebrate the progress, and about a year later they survey the employees yet again. Connecting the dots after the third survey, senior leaders now have a trend line for employee engagement, one of the few truly forward-looking indices of business health.

In addition to informing better decisions, data should give leaders greater confidence in the actions they take. This is also true for managers, who, according to the research we have referenced in earlier chapters, are usually not well equipped to elicit high levels of engagement from their teams. But we have seen something quite remarkable in our client companies[85] as they celebrate their progress every year. Managers approach us and say, "I was skeptical when we started working with you because we have cycled through leadership fads over the years. But this really works. My scores went up and I can track why they went up." This is a remarkable confidence builder for leaders and managers who are struggling to juggle their career-based skill sets (as an engineer, doctor, accountant) with their role as manager and leader now responsible for the wildly variant examples of workplace performance, behavior, and attitudes. My experience is that great managers like having science-based metrics that help guide them toward being a better leader.

---

reasonable in a workplace social ecosystem. For comparison, most of our client companies report between 40 and 50 percent engagement in their baseline year.

85 E3 Solutions' clients represent a broad cross section of the American economy, from the Fortune 100 to the Fortune 5000, including large pharma, a consortium of over eighty acute care hospitals, technology manufacturers, service and engineering firms, public utilities, and nonprofits.

ENGAGEMENT DISTRIBUTION: COMPARATIVE ANALYSIS

E3 Solutions cumulative global data

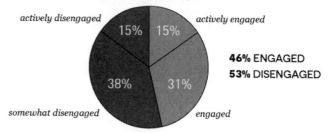

actively disengaged   *actively engaged*

15%   15%

38%   31%

46% ENGAGED
53% DISENGAGED

somewhat disengaged   *engaged*

When organizations become intentional about creating workplace conditions where employees will thrive by design, they see significant changes year-over-year. Looking at our clients with a minimum of four contiguous annual surveys, we see significant improvement year-over-year.

survey year 1

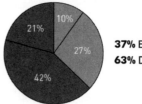

21%   10%

27%

42%

37% ENGAGED
63% DISENGAGED

survey year 2

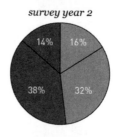

14%   16%

38%   32%

48% ENGAGED
52% DISENGAGED

survey year 3

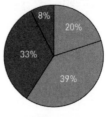

8%   20%

33%

39%

59% ENGAGED
41% DISENGAGED

survey year 4

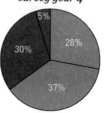

5%   26%

30%

37%

65% ENGAGED
35% DISENGAGED

When you measure engagement, aggregate the data, and then share it with managers in the organization, it is important to establish a positive frame (identifying "opportunities," not "weakness"). You are searching for ways to encourage a high-performance culture rather than looking for employees to punish. You want managers embracing the process instead of viewing it as a threat.

Having their performance assessed across a range of factors that feels new (this isn't in my job description), somewhat awkward (I don't come to work to build relationships), and even tangential (we don't need to celebrate—this is a job) can be daunting. It can also feel like a new paradigm for leadership, one they never signed up for. And as in all systems based on a meritocracy, many managers will feel uncomfortable when their performance is compared to others in the organization. Managers who score well typically feel validated and grateful; managers who score poorly often have feelings that range from inadequacy (I knew I shouldn't have taken a managerial position) to a lack of fairness (those other leaders have it easier than I do) and relevance (I hit my production targets, what else do they want?). In extreme cases, we have seen leaders and managers scorn the process itself, attacking the tool and those delivering it.

SHARING THE DATA ACROSS THE ENTERPRISE

Whatever tool you used to measure workplace engagement, the essential next step is to work with the data to identify the what, where, and with whom? What is working, and what needs attention? Where in the organization do we see the highest levels of employee engagement, and where in the organization do we see the lowest? Which managers are the positive deviants in the organization, and which managers are struggling and need help?

The most important trend to look for is each company's growth and improvement internally, not how they compare with others. There are some very popular surveys used nationwide where organizations are benchmarked against each other. We have found that while companies love participating and sharing their results when they're at the top of the pile, they lose enthusiasm as they drop down the totem pole of popularity. What's most disheartening in this process is that they often are making great strides internally but their success is overshadowed by their public standing against other organizations.

Managing this process of sharing the data is just as important as the decision to collect it in the first place. Employees want to know the results because they care about the organization, they want to know the views of their peers, and they want to make sure their voices are heard, among other reasons. Transparency with the data (typically at the organizational level, not manager by manager[86]) creates goodwill and momentum for positive change.

Here is the most effective formula we have found for releasing the data to employees:

I. **Release the results.**

    When employees participate in a survey, they expect to see the results. This is best accomplished by sharing the data for the organization as a whole, indicating what percentage of employees are actively disengaged, somewhat disengaged, engaged, and actively engaged. This is often difficult for some leaders to do, because in their first year the results almost always fall below their expectations. The way the

---

86 The first step in sharing the data is to release it to the entire organization. This is best accomplished at a very high level—for example, the entire organization's score benchmarked against E3's global database. The managerial level and individual workgroup results should be discussed in one-on-one meetings. In subsequent years, we find the best comparison is the year-over-year data for that organization.

data is framed is critical, and we will elaborate on that later in this section.

II. **Identify key themes.**

Senior leaders should identify three themes they "heard" in the data (the voice of employees). Our suggestion is to always start with something that ranked high in the survey. Of the variables we track, "proud to work for this organization" almost always ranks number one. It is important to begin with a finding that represents a strength of the organization. In communicating the results to employees, for example, the CEO could say, "As a leadership team, we were very grateful to see that the highest-ranking item in the survey was the fact that employees are proud to work for our organization."

The second key theme that leadership recognizes from the survey data would ideally be something related to either the organization's mission or core values. A statement here could be something like "And as an organization that believes strongly in mutual respect as one of our core values, we were gratified to see that the fourth highest-ranking item in the survey was that employees feel valued for more than the work they produce. We will work hard over the coming year to move this score even higher."

The third theme that leadership highlights from survey results should come from the lowest-ranking variables, the biggest opportunities for the organization going forward. In almost all cases, the cluster of lowest-ranking items in our employee engagement survey relate to validation, recognition, and feedback. Framing this low-scoring factor in a proactive way is critical. The CEO might say something like "And one of the biggest opportunities we have as an organization is to improve the way we value and recognize employees at all levels in the organization. That message was received loud and clear."

III. **Commit to taking action.**

The employees now know there is transparency around the data, and they know their voices have been heard. The third step is for leadership to publicly commit to action steps based on the data. These actions could correspond with the three themes previously outlined (although they don't need to).

For example, senior leaders could announce the following:

First theme: "As we talked about the high score related to pride in working for Globex, we realized we have not celebrated as a company in quite some time for all we have accomplished. We have decided to have an all-hands company event on Friday morning, June 15, to acknowledge the great accomplishments of our staff. The meeting will end with a catered lunch and an early end to the day."

Second theme: "We were excited to see the high score on how employees feel valued here at Globex, especially because it supports our core value of mutual respect. We want to do a better job of highlighting the importance of this core value by starting a Spirit of Respect award that we will give quarterly based on nominations from employees."

Third theme: "We know we can do a better job in how we validate and recognize employees and how we offer feedback. As a result, within the next month we will announce a group comprised of employees at all levels of the organization who will focus on new ideas for how we validate and recognize our outstanding employees. We will ask that group to complete their assignment as soon as possible so we can tell you the actions we will implement immediately thereafter."

Why is it so important to release results in this manner? Even when results are shared at the highest aggregation level—the entire company—it promotes transparency, understanding, and a commitment to continuous improvement in culture and teamwork. When organizations do a survey and then don't share the results, the impact on the organization is negative. Employees feel left in the dark. They either perceive that the results don't actually matter ("Nothing is going to change." "Waste of time." "My voice wasn't heard.") or that the results were so terrible that senior leadership is too embarrassed to release them. That leaves a negative impression and has an unhealthy impact on employee engagement. When the survey is regularly implemented and results are shared, it becomes more credible to employees, especially when changes are made to the organization based on input received through the tool.

Performing the survey year after year also encourages leaders to become more comfortable focusing on what have traditionally been called "soft skills." When it comes to dealing with employees, leaders need to use or develop relational skills in order to connect with employees at an emotional level. Often this leaves leaders feeling nervous or uncertain; few of them were mentored in these skills, so implementing them in the workplace feels awkward. However, when the scores from their survey show improvement, leaders feel validated and recognized for their efforts to make changes. By the second year of the survey, leaders begin to see that the efforts are working, and they really start to commit and engage in the process.

Without measuring, organizations have no true indicators of whether actions are working—whether they're really moving the needle toward engagement. Demonstrating with data that the efforts are working encourages participation. By the third year of the process, most leaders are true believers because they really see the value of the data and they can see that the process works. Those managers who don't opt in, who continue on their way without making changes, may even see their indicators go down. This process captures not only early adopters but also leaders who are trying, and identifies those who aren't progressing or are moving the needle backward. Measurement is a cornerstone in creating this shift. When our clients implement the changes we recommend, with consistency and rigor, employees across the enterprise move to higher levels of engagement.

While releasing the data to employees is best done at the organizational level, the debriefs for individual divisions, regions, or manager workgroups should be done in smaller settings. Most of our clients provide debriefs for individual managers privately.[87] The objective here is not to embarrass individual managers but to let them know where they stand compared to their peers, what is possible, their leading strengths, and their biggest opportunities. The focus should be proactive and aspirational, encouraging them to achieve significant improvement in the following year's survey.

---

87 At the departmental level, the aggregated workgroup results can be compared to the company averages. Typically, only the senior leadership team looks at the workgroup-by-workgroup data.

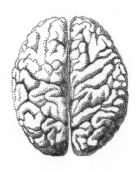

CHAPTER INSIGHTS

→ Leaders can support and encourage a high-performance culture by using data related to employee engagement to identify critical opportunities and outline action steps for manager development.

→ Engagement data identifies a baseline of employee engagement in the first instance, and then, at each recurrence (typically annually), the data highlights progress, what is possible, and what opportunities remain. As scores improve each year, managers are validated for their efforts and commitment and encouraged to accomplish more.

→ Sharing engagement data at a high level with employees is a critical part of the measuring process. When senior leaders release the results, they should identify three key themes they "heard" in the data (the voice of employees) and commit to taking a few action steps based on the insights gained from the employees.

CHAPTER ACTION STEPS

→ *Reflect:* When my organization collects employee engagement data (from any source), are we making the most use of it? Are we, as leaders, too focused on the tactical "fixes" like action plans, and hitting engagement "targets," when the pivotal issues are more about the emotional aspects of the human condition—namely, the need to have trusted social resources, job and mission clarity, and a relational culture where employees are seen, valued, and recognized?

→ *Act:* If your organization does not have employee engagement data, explore options to conduct a survey across the enterprise. Contact E3 Solutions for more information on our E3A engagement survey.

→ *Quick Win:* E3 Solutions' proprietary engagement survey can do this for you right away. Reach out to hello@ e3solutions to set up a consultation and start measuring your engagement initiatives.

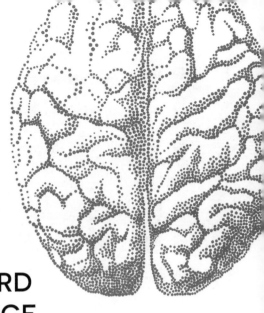

CHAPTER 11

MOVING FORWARD WITH THE SCIENCE OF LEADERSHIP

The way to get started is to quit talking and begin doing.
—WALT DISNEY

For too long, employers worldwide have been looking for solutions to common workplace challenges such as absenteeism, low productivity, and the ability to attract and retain top talent. Decades of research have shown that the path to solving these issues lies in developing a strong foundation of intentional leadership based on empirically validated theories of human behavior. Most companies do not have the personnel, experience, and thorough content understanding to initiate an efficient and effective employee engagement program that ties together the science, the training materials, and the experiential learning. When employee engagement initiatives have to be created and sustained with internal resources alone, we have seen the difficulties in getting started, as members of the staff wonder:

❓ What really works?

❓ What should we do first?

❓ Who will create the materials?

❓ How do we ensure a common organizing principle to all the training?

❓ What is the best way to embed the learning?

❓ How will we measure success?

The good news is that you don't have to do this important work alone! We know that leaders' agendas are already overpacked. That is why my team is available to support you as you move forward in implementing what you've learned throughout this book.

E3 Solutions is a fast-growing consultancy specializing in science-based approaches to accurately measure and improve levels of employee engagement. E3 uses proven methods to build sustainable and impactful leadership practices for companies of all sizes and industries. Here is a compilation of resources for your reference and recommended use to develop your own foundation in science-based leadership.

ONLINE RESOURCES

Two of the most important steps leaders can take to support sustained employee engagement are to measure engagement regularly and to surround managers with support as they foster highly engaged teams. Here are a few ways we can help with your organization:

Manager Resource Center

At the end of each chapter of the book, you've seen me reference valuable resources that serve as strategic action steps for you to implement what you have learned. All of these tools and many more are found in our Manager Resource Center. This comprehensive leadership platform allows you to surround yourself and your organization with resources that grow dynamic and highly engaged teams. The platform includes three high-level sections: *Foundation* (the building blocks of employee engagement), *Next Level Leadership* (focusing on your team), and *Lifelong Leadership* (focusing on yourself). Customize your leadership journey by exploring a myriad of topics within each section at your own pace and direction. Content is regularly updated and includes a variety of articles, videos, tools, self-assessments, and more. Every week, we send participants an email with a specific leadership topic to focus on, including an article to read and a tool to implement, to help leaders be as intentional and focused as possible with their teams. You can learn more about this resource at ManagerResourceCenter.com.

E3A Tool

As you read in chapters 9 and 10, the importance of measuring and making use of solid data is essential. E3 Solutions' assessment tool, the E3A, is a research-driven, online diagnostic tool that helps CEOs and their leadership team get a clear and accurate picture of their organization's engagement levels. It measures the quality of the relationships between supervisors and the employees who report to them; it can identify critical shortfalls in performance, behaviors, and productivity well before your customers feel their impact.

Our team of experts analyzes the survey results to deliver an accurate picture of your organization's strengths and most important opportunities. Our E3A clients also have access to a cloud-based portal that provides full reports and tips on what individual managers can do to improve their scores. The E3A is the only organizational diagnostic tool of its kind that will:

- ✅ focus on relational drivers of exemplary behavior
- ✅ identify critical problem areas by manager, team, division, or region
- ✅ offer additional insight based on tenure, age, and gender cohort
- ✅ provide detailed, forward-looking indicators for critical business metrics like productivity, profitability, and the customer experience
- ✅ deliver actionable results in real time

IN-PERSON RESOURCES

Another great way to introduce a system-wide shift in employee engagement is to bring all your leaders together to spend dedicated time learning about the science that drives employee engagement and collectively focus on critical topics for your organization. Here is a list of all the in-person workshops we host with companies of all sizes that offer an opportunity to get everyone on the same page about the importance of engagement.

WORKSHOPS

Employee Engagement Boot Camp for Managers

The Employee Engagement Boot Camp for Managers is our cornerstone workshop. Offer your managers new skills for increasing staff engagement and a deeper understanding of employee performance dynamics. This highly rated workshop offers immediately actionable takeaways and is the foundation of our work with managers to help them develop exceptional leadership skills. It is an essential building block for enabling new behaviors based on our proven Neural Alignment™ process for managers and leaders or a starting point for our work with managers on developing leadership skills that promote an engaged workforce.

Accountability Workshop

Accountability is a key pillar of every high-performance culture. Employees need to be committed to their own accountability and insist on it with their colleagues. The ability to have accountability conversations with each other in a curious, collaborative, and safe fashion is a critical skill for managers. This session guides leaders through the process of having difficult conversations and holding people accountable without the typical negative sting and punitive demeanor.

Effective Communication Workshop

One of the most common themes raised in the open-ended comments made by employees who take our E3A is the need for more and better communication. Employees ask for more effective communication from their leaders and more opportunities to communicate among and between teams. This half-day workshop focuses on improving both professional and interpersonal communication skills for managers. As one of our original workshops, we have provided this session to a wide range of clients ranging from the National Institutes of Health (NIH), the Securities and Exchange Commission (SEC), and Fortune 100 company clients.

Emotional Intelligence Workshop

Emotional intelligence (EQ) is a set of emotional and social skills that influence the way we perceive and express ourselves, develop and maintain social relationships, cope with challenges, and use emotional information in an effective and meaningful way. EQ is an indicator for leadership success. Research links emotional intelligence to higher sales and profits, increased performance, improved customer satisfaction, decreased attrition rates, and reduced training costs. Emotional intelligence is not a static factor—it can change over time and be developed in targeted areas. The key to success is identifying the behaviors we want to improve in order to be a better leader.

Extraordinary Workplace Summit for Employees

In most cases, especially when employee engagement levels are low, the most effective way to support rapid improvement is to supplement manager-focused training with a hands-on experience for employees. Our Extraordinary Workplace Summit helps employees focus on what they envision as a great workplace (values, behaviors, relationships) and then on what steps are needed to achieve that ideal workplace culture. To keep the interaction positive and productive, this session is aspirational, forward looking, and focuses on existing strengths. This workshop is a perfect complement to our Employee Engagement Boot Camp for Managers.

Finding Meaning & Purpose Workshop

Employees, especially millennials, are more engaged in their work and the company's mission when they find meaning and purpose in what they do every day. Whenever employers focus more strategically on the meaning and purpose that employees find in their work, workplace engagement increases. This half-day workshop helps managers (1) learn how to identify the meaning and purpose their direct reports find in their work, (2) help develop a sense of meaning and purpose for those employees with only a nascent understanding of the larger implications of what they do, and (3) learn how to incorporate these values-based motivations and intrinsic drivers of engagement into their leadership strategy.

Leading Effective Meetings Workshop

This workshop was initially developed for one of the world's most successful broadcast corporations because of the high cost (wasted staff time, employee frustration, and inefficient decision making) of substandard professionalism in running meetings. The workshop offers a wide range of techniques and practical advice on how to run more effective meetings. The net result is fewer meetings of shorter duration where more work is accomplished. In workplaces where employees frequently comment on a lack of time and too many meetings, this workshop provides welcome relief.

Positive Leadership Workshop

Give managers a deep dive into the practical science of positive leadership and why it works. Positive leadership is the strategic reliance on a positive bias to support employee well-being, improve business outcomes like productivity and profitability, and create better alignment within organizations. Research on a range of companies shows positive leadership practices leading to remarkable and immediate shifts in leader effectiveness and employee performance. In order to create the most effective, tailored seminar for your managers, E3 conducts a twenty-two-question assessment on positive leadership prior to or during the seminar. Participants learn important new developments in the science of positive leadership and develop a road map for how they can incorporate these valuable insights into their leadership style and performance.

Recognition & Feedback Workshop

Human beings are hardwired at a neurological level to care about how they are valued by others, both consciously and subconsciously. Managers who consistently provide positive, detailed, and substantive recognition and feedback to their team members typically support higher levels of employee engagement. In this half-day workshop, we review the science supporting the most effective techniques for providing feedback and recognition. In addition, managers will be given a range of skills and practical examples that can be put to immediate use.

The Science of Motivation Workshop

Outcomes depend as much, if not more, on the quality of motivation than the quantity. The traditional carrot-and-stick way of motivating quickly fades. Managers find out too late that once the stimulus is removed, an employee's personal battery seems to die. We take a deep dive into the science of motivation that lies behind ambition, accountability, awareness, and agility and the counterproductive behaviors that may be holding them hostage. This workshop helps provide the tools you need to unlock the key to motivation.

Executive Coaching

We take a holistic approach to coaching executives, focusing on the individual leader as well as their surrounding support system. We diagnose target behavioral habits that need improvement. Then we forge a path to growth that involves the feedback and input of stakeholders who provide ongoing accountability and support. The end result is long-term, measurable change in behaviors that make you, the team, and your organization stronger. Our executive coaching process will increase your power and effectiveness to help you achieve peak performance. Together we will determine long-term goals based on your personal vision, strengths, and motivations. Then we'll conduct a position analysis to help determine the direction of your growth in the organization, with a focus on changing the agreed-upon leadership behaviors.

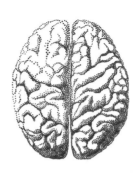

CHAPTER INSIGHTS

➴ There are practical, proven, and easily accessible options for leaders to begin the journey to a high-performance culture, where employees look forward to coming to work every day.

➴ Organizations have options to measure, to offer new skills (through workshops), and to provide 24/7 support to managers through online resources targeted to their most persistent needs.

➴ E3 Solutions is a trusted partner in making science-based, data-driven, consistent, and significant improvements in employee engagement.

CHAPTER ACTION STEPS

➴ *Reflect:* Where does your team need the most help in improving engagement and fostering a high-performance culture? Do you need to surround yourself or your leaders with ongoing support and leadership tools? Do you need your team to improve their skills on accountability, communication, or positive leadership?

How can you support your organization by equipping them with online or in-person resources?

→ *Act:* Identify at least one way you can take a step closer to gaining a highly engaged workforce. Whether it's measuring engagement, surrounding yourself with leadership tools and resources, or participating in a seminar to offer better skills, reach out to E3 Solutions and see how we can help you. Explore everything we have to offer at www.e3solutions.com.

→ *Not yet a Manager Resource Center subscriber?* Visit ManagerResourceCenter.com to learn more and sign up.

→ You might also be interested in booking Don Rheem for a *Thrive by Design* event involving your leadership team, an all-employee meeting, or with a professional organization for your industry. Please contact hello@e3solutions.com.

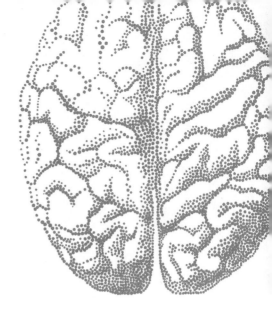

EPILOGUE

Thank you for sharing your time with this book and learning about our approach to encouraging healthier, happier, and more rewarding high-performance workplace cultures. We know firsthand the differences the insights contained in these pages can make when organizational leaders commit to a science-based, focused set of interventions that not only let managers know what they should do but also why the actions are so effective. Some of what you read here may have felt familiar and perhaps even like common sense—but please remember this—common sense is not common practice. I hope you commit to be intentional around your culture in order to offer employees a safe haven workplace where they can *Thrive by Design!*

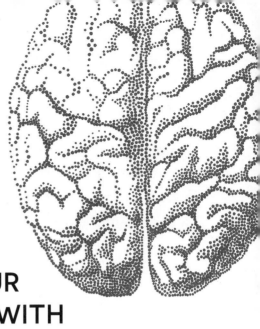

MEASURING YOUR ORGANIZATION WITH THE E3A

REPORTING THE DATA

As an example, an organization with five hundred employees might have fifty people in leadership positions (from supervisors up to the senior leadership team) in three locations. The organization might have four functional areas, including marketing, manufacturing, sales, and back office (accounting and HR). Our assessment tool measures engagement at every level of the organization: company wide, region, division, team, and manager. To achieve this, we divide your organization into workgroups, defined as any group of five or more employees who report to the same manager. Physical location, department, job, and title are not factors, but who provides their daily direction and regular feedback is.

The organization's survey org chart (something we prepare for each client) might look like what you see on page 214. If all fifty managers have at least five people reporting to them, there will be a total of fifty workgroups measured. Each of these managers will receive their own E3A report identifying which employee engagement categories their direct reports fall into, from the actively disengaged to the actively engaged.

At the same time, the fifty workgroups can be rolled up into three virtual workgroups, one for each of the locations. The fifty workgroups can also be rolled up into the four functional areas. In this kind of a reporting matrix, senior leaders can quickly see that the manufacturing workgroups at a particular location need immediate attention and that the accounting staff in the corporate office is highly engaged. They can also drill down into the individual workgroup data to get a better idea of the most urgent opportunities.

Areas measured in the E3A:

1. Assessed against measurable targets

2. Alignment with organization's goals

3. Monthly progress/performance discussions

4. Using your strengths at work

5. Expectations

6. Recognition

7. Appreciation

8. Feeling valued

9. Encouragement and support

10. Opinions encouraged and matter

11. Contributing to organization goals

12. Proud to work for this organization

13. Work tasks are challenging

14. Senior leaders' behavior is consistent with mission, vision, and values

15. Celebrating employee accomplishments

16. Tolerating poor performance

17. Input on decisions

18. Working well together as a team

19. Treated as valued partners

20. Respect and trust

21. Cooperation from other teams

22. Pride in work

23. Resources

24. Treated fairly by supervisor

25. Training

26. Trusted friend at work

27. Respect and trust for supervisor

28. Treated fairly by the organization

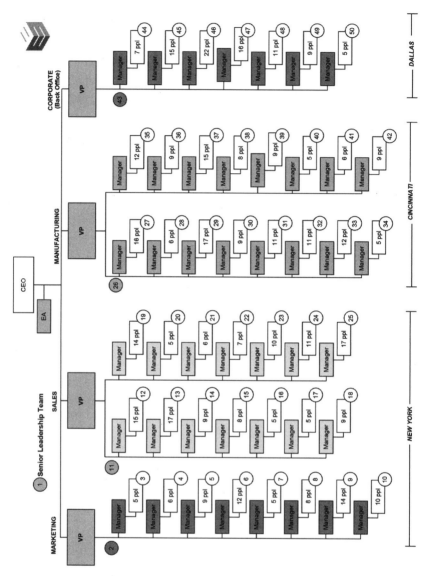

Creating an organizational chart that identifies managers with at least five people reporting to them is the first step in preparing for a client survey. In this example, there are fifty workgroups ranging from the senior leadership team (Workgroup 1) to the manager in Dallas (Workgroup 50) with only five staff. Workgroups can be bundled to show, for example, how staff members in different locations compare to each other. (See Workgroups 2, 11, 26, and 43.) The more specific the data, the better, so some clients will take a large workgroup like Workgroup 46 and break it down further. In this example, there might be three or four supervisors in Workgroup 46 with at least five staff members, so three or four more workgroups could be created.

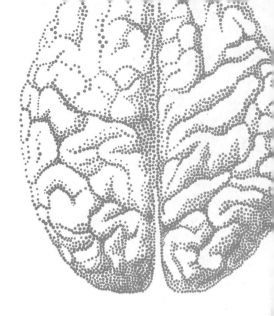

INDEX